Cheap and Cheerful
Homemaking on a budget

CHEAP AND CHEERFUL

HOMEMAKING ON A BUDGET

ANNE FORSYTH

Illustrated by Patty Johns

MILLS & BOON LIMITED, London

First published in Great Britain 1973 by Mills & Boon
Limited, 17–19 Foley Street, London W1A 1DR.

ISBN 0 263 05236 2

Made and Printed in Great Britain by
Clarke, Doble & Brendon Limited,
Plymouth

CONTENTS

1 Introduction 7

2 Planning the colour scheme 10

3 The living-room 18

4 The bedroom 34

5 The hall and entrance 44

6 The kitchen 49

7 The bathroom 55

8 Paint and paper 58

9 The extras 68

10 The front door 76

11 Value for money 83

12 Taking measurements 88

13 Tools 95

14 Book list 97

15 Where to find out about . . . 99

Index 103

1 INTRODUCTION

You've signed the contract, paid the deposit, settled with the surveyor
—and now you are ready to begin decorating and furnishing your
first home. It is fairly certain that your first home will be a modest
dwelling. This is not a book for those who have the energy or resources to
convert an oast house or disused railway station into a beautiful
and unusual home. It is for the first-time owner, and especially
the woman on her own, who has limited time, skill and very limited
resources.

It's also likely that your first home will be in a modern development
housing scheme or a council house. Perhaps it is a two-bedroomed
maisonette, the ground-floor flat in a block or the top flat in a skyscraper
tower. But wherever it is, your new home will probably have exactly
the same layout, design and outward appearance as fifty-odd others
in the scheme.

For, no matter how you hanker after the unusual Victorian terraced
house 'in need of some decoration', as advertisements often say,
you soon come to realise that this is rarely a practical proposition for
the inexperienced first home owner. The surveyor's report (always
essential, even with a new house) often reveals dry rot, rising damp and
antiquated wiring behind that attractive façade. It is hard enough to
obtain a mortgage on new property and even more difficult when it
comes to older houses. So it is sound business sense to buy a relatively
problem-free modern house for your first home, especially if you have
just enough money for the deposit and don't want to involve yourself in
endless financial worries over the cost of structural repairs.

By the time you have found the deposit, paid the legal fees, arranged
the move, and finally watched the removal men dump the last box in the

middle of the empty floor, there is not likely to be much money to spare (and indeed, you may be glad of those packing cases as extra chairs and table).

So all the way through this book we shall be looking at ways to furnish cheaply, at the very lowest price and the best value. By shopping around, buying secondhand and careful planning of your budget, it can be done. Of course, if you want to budget for a major buy (say a carpet or sofa, which you feel you must have right away), then you will have to scrimp on other things. How you plan your priorities is your business. But a word of warning. Don't try to buy too much at first. If you rush into a purchase about which you feel uncertain, then your first doubts will soon become real dislike for the purchase. You may easily change your mind about a colour scheme later on or find that the sofa you bought doesn't really fit into the room.

And while you are gradually accumulating pieces of furniture don't be discouraged because you haven't a home as well furnished as your neighbour's. Buy what you want, when you can afford it. If you can't run to fitted carpets for years, it doesn't matter. There are other ways of covering floors.

Ideas come cheapest of all, and you can find them anywhere. It is the imaginative touches that make a home, not the expensive ones.

One of the most attractive homes I've seen was created by a girl working to the tightest possible budget. The main room has sanded floors, a joiner's workbench for a table, chairs which she bought at a junk shop and stripped and painted green, bench seating picked up cheaply and covered with foam rubber and bright cushions. Nothing cost over £3·50, and by learning to carry out such tasks as stripping wood, sanding, painting and decorating, she has saved a fortune.

In this book we will concentrate on the basic jobs that any fumble-fisted amateur can do alone. It is almost impossible now to find the small builder or carpenter who will do such modest jobs as putting up fitments and some decorating. If you do find him, he is a treasure indeed. (See chapter 6.) There are a good many jobs, however, that you can manage on your own, though I would exclude electrical work and putting up shelves. Various local authorities and organisations such as the Electrical

Association for Women run excellent courses on simple electrical housecraft, but I'm sure they would all agree that it is dangerous to tackle such tasks as wiring or altering fittings, especially in a house which is unfamiliar. Shelving too, should be put up by someone who really knows what he is doing, as every shelf has to bear more weight than you think, and shelves must be firmly fixed to the walls.

But the basic do-it-yourself jobs are easier than they look. You will save a great deal of money if you learn to Rawlplug walls, put up curtain fitments and strip furniture. The assistants at your local do-it-yourself shop will explain how to use any equipment you buy. And if you have any query about the instructions given with a piece of equipment or a kit, write to the manufacturer or call at the showroom.

When you are planning your home, kind friends and relatives may offer you pieces of furniture—perhaps a large wardrobe, or a chest of drawers that just goes through the front door. If the furniture isn't what you want, it is going to be difficult to get it out of the door again. You're going to hate that vast wardrobe when it comes to cleaning, or the large settee when you want lots of extra space. It is better to be firm (but kind and tactful) and realistic about such gifts, and say no thank you. This is your home, and you can afford time to save and choose.

2 PLANNING THE COLOUR SCHEME

Before you start decorating and furnishing, you must plan your colour scheme. Even if you have never furnished a room before, with care and forethought you can confidently be your own designer.

The secret of planning a colour scheme is to choose your main colour or pattern and build round that. If you have decided to buy a carpet, this is a major buy and it is wise to select the carpet colour first and design the rest of the room around it. In a room which will not be dominated by the carpet colour, you could link your scheme to wallpaper or curtains or a bright paint colour, and match rugs, cushions and extras. There are a few basic rules about colour planning. Generally it is a mistake to mix patterns in a room. It takes a skilled designer to make this look intentional and it is usually much better and more restful on the eye to use one patterned fabric or paper only, and pick out the main colours from that pattern to use in the other furnishings.

Before you choose colours, it is wise to take a good look at your room several times during the day. Many rooms in small modern flats are rather dark and poky. It is important to avoid choosing a colour which will be overpowering and claustrophobic late in the day, by artificial light or on a dull day. It's wise to remember this when looking at the shade cards because it is so easy to be carried away by the splendidly subtle and trendy new paint shades, and use them in the wrong way.

If you have doubts, do try out one wall in your chosen colour. Often you can live with one dramatic wall when four would be overpowering. For example, if you fancy a deep cinnamon, try it first on one wall only with the other three in ivory. You could try a deep turquoise with three white walls, or a deep candy pink with three walls of a pale grey. It is essential to use the same tone. You would not, for example, have a gold wall with a straw yellow or hot Italian pink with a soft pastel pink.

People often quote such rules as 'don't use blues and greens in a north-facing room', but of course any rules can be broken, and there is no reason why you shouldn't use blue or green if you select the right shades and add warmth in the furnishings.

If you have a lot of prints and pictures to display, it is wise to keep the walls a fairly pale shade, to show pictures to best advantage. You can't go wrong with white.

Before you start furnishing the room, it is a good idea to plan it in miniature. Collect scraps of material from the ragbag, snippets of fabric from manufacturers' samples, pieces of wallpaper, carpet samples, and try your hand at planning a room on paper.

Don't worry if you aren't very expert at drawing.You can easily mark out the plan of your room with the height and width in proportion. Mark in the windows and the doors and any other features such as fireplace.

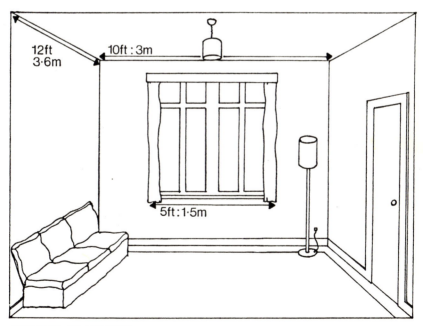

COLOUR PLANNING

Fig 1   A living-room plan.

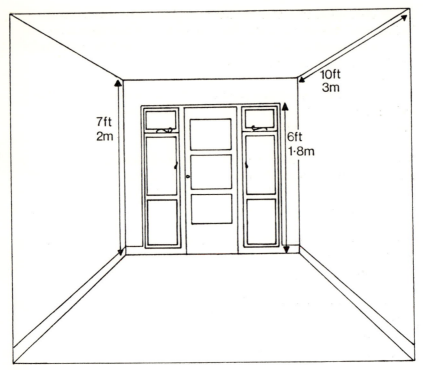

10ft
3m

7ft
2m

6ft
1·8m

Fig 2   A dining alcove plan.

Note any furniture which you already have. Make a note of the way
the room faces, and decide on your main colour or dominating pattern.
Build up the scheme with samples of wallpaper, curtain fabric of your
choice, carpet or rug, and pieces of fabric or snippets of coloured paper
for the extras such as lampshades and cushions. If you glue these snippets
on to a piece of plain white card, you can note the room's measurements
on the back of the card, and take it with you as a handy guide when
you go shopping.

If you want to make a rather more detailed scheme, you can make your
drawing large enough to glue the snippets on to the plan itself and this
will give you a fairly good idea of how the room will look as a whole.

It is fun, and good practice in designing, to work out several schemes
using the same basic key fabric or wallpaper. For example, you may think
of using a pink candy-striped wallpaper as the main feature in a bedroom.

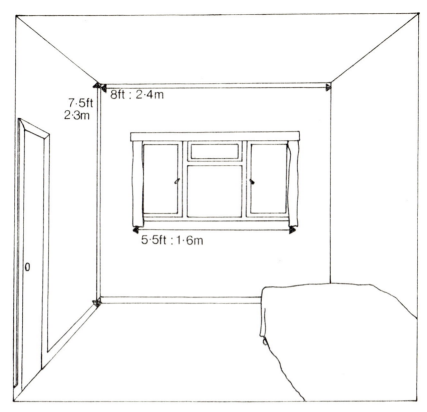

Fig 3 A bedroom plan.

Perhaps you would choose matching curtains in the same fabric, with
plain pink braid trimming, or perhaps you would choose a self-coloured
candy pink cotton or crisp white cotton seersucker. On the floor you
might use deep pink or white cotton rugs. You might choose a white
honeycomb cotton bedspread or a cotton lace spread with a deep pink
sheet underneath, and complete the furnishings with a wicker chair and
deep pink and mauve cushions. But if you were using the same paper in a
sitting-room, it might look too light and feminine. So you could use the
striped paper on one wall only, and paint the other three walls in a
matching pink. You could choose grey carpeting, white or pale grey
paintwork, heavy repp curtains in a deep pink, and cushions and other
accessories in a deep strong pink and purple.

B

It is interesting to plan a number of schemes on paper before you decide
on the one you want. If you do have a particular colour in mind, say
yellow, it is useful to gather a selection of fabrics and papers in different
yellows, so that you can choose the shades best suited to your room.
Here are a few ideas to help you begin planning colour schemes. They
are of course only suggestions and you will be able to think up many
more ideas yourself.

BLUE

For a south- or west-facing room you can have any shade of blue—ice blue
if you want. For a *south-facing* room, an attractive scheme would be
pale blue walls, deep mauve curtains, grey carpet, white paintwork and
dark wood furniture. The dark wood helps you to avoid too feminine
or fragile a look.

For a *west-facing room* you could choose : pale lilac walls, deeper
lilac curtains, grey carpet, grey and white paintwork and again dark
wood furniture.

North- and east-facing rooms are slightly more difficult to plan, but here
the secret is to introduce warm tones wherever you can. For example, in
a *north-facing* room, you could have blue walls in a hyacinth tone which
is warmer than a pale blue, blue-grey patterned curtains, deep blue
carpet, pale grey paint, dark wood furniture and use a warm rose colour
for cushions and other extras.

The same idea about the warmer tones of blue applies to the scheme for
an *east-facing room*. Here you could choose hyacinth blue walls, deep
plum curtains, white rugs on the floor, white paintwork, dark wood
furniture and the same shade of deep plum for cushions and extras.

Natural wood furniture always looks attractive in a modern home, but
with blues it tends to look rather cold, whereas with yellows it brings out
the warmth of the colour. And if you are buying secondhand—see the
next chapter—you will find it easier to buy dark furniture than light.
The light wood furniture in secondhand shops tends to look rather
cheap and reminiscent of the utility furniture of the late 1940s.

RED

This includes all shades from bright red to soft pink, and in a south- or west-facing room, you can happily use the softer pinks, while a north- or east-facing room demands more vivid colours.

A *south-facing* room could have pale pink walls, deeper pink curtains, pale grey carpet, white paintwork and a very deep turquoise for cushions and extras so that the room doesn't look too pale and uninteresting.

A *west-facing* room could have deeper pink paint on the walls, a pink and brown mosaic print for the curtains, a soft brown for the carpet, with white gloss paint for the doors and skirting boards. Here the choice of furniture may be dark or light wood.

North- and east-facing rooms can be decorated with the most vivid shades of red. With a *north-facing* room you could choose a simple scheme of white paint on the walls, dark cerise curtains, white rugs on the floor and matching red upholstery. Remember that if you are using a very vivid red for the curtains, a background of white walls looks clean and cool and avoids any over-fussy effect. For an *east-facing* room I would suggest white paint on the walls, jazzy scarlet and orange curtains, rush matting for the floor and bright scarlet painted furniture. You would of course have white gloss paintwork throughout.

GREEN

A word of warning. Unless you have a special yearning for it, try to avoid that anonymous apple green so beloved of public halls and offices. It does nothing for a room and when it gets dirty, it looks grubbier than any other colour. The greens run the gamut from lime green to deep turquoise, and lime is a good colour for a modern house. In a *south-* or *west-facing* room you could have lime walls, lime printed curtains, coffee-coloured carpet or rush matting on the floor, and white gloss paintwork with natural tones for furniture and extras. I have also seen a very successful combination of lime, tangerine and white. In this case, you could have the walls white, curtains lime, rugs in deep tangerine and lime with natural wood or wicker furniture.

If you are wary of using too bright a lime, try it on one wall only—I've
seen this work very well in a west-facing sitting-room. The room had
three walls white and the fourth a vivid lime green, with natural rush
matting and natural weave curtains. To pick up the lime green on the wall
there were two inexpensive prints of birds—a whitethroat and a linnet.

YELLOW

You can't go wrong whatever the aspect of your room. There is only
one rule, and that is not to mix your yellows. Orange kills a lime yellow
stone dead. A deep tawny gold looks wrong with a straw yellow.

In a *south-* or *west-facing* room you can use lots of white with the yellow.
Here a good scheme would be white walls, white for paintwork,
buttercup yellow curtains, white rugs and natural or dark wood as you
prefer.

In a *north-* or *east-facing* room you can use deep orange shades. You
could have three walls white, one deep tangerine, tangerine print curtains,
natural wood furniture, and rush matting on the floor, with white
paintwork. Or you could choose white walls, plain tawny gold curtains
and a deep gold carpet, and patterned extras in a tawny gold print. For
a really vivid splash of colour you could try white walls, orange
curtains, white knock-down furniture, and extras in orange, pink or red.

In all these schemes I haven't specified paint or paper because this is very
much a matter of individual taste. When it comes to cost there is no
great difference in the price. You will find a table at the end of the book,
giving guidance on how much paper and paint you will need.

Whether you are buying paint or wallpaper, remember to buy enough
for the whole job, because it is often difficult to match the paper or shade
of paint afterwards.

And when buying paints, do be careful about those which are mixed to a
particular shade by your paint stockist. This is not an aspersion on the
dealer, but you must remember that paint on the shade card, or even
the tin, can look very different in another light, or even when it is spread

over a very large area. What you thought was a singing pink in the
shop can turn out to be a screaming puce on the wall. So it is often
better to choose a shade slightly paler than the one you originally selected
from the shade card.

If you mix your own paint, it is a wise precaution to write out the recipe
and keep it in a safe place, or you will spend a great deal of time trying
to remember how you did it last time. Generally speaking, paint mixing
is not too difficult, but it can be wasteful, and if you want to try your
hand at it, it's best to experiment with a small quantity first and make
sure that you get the proportions correct.

3 THE LIVING~ROOM

The living-room is the most important room in the house. You will spend most of your waking hours there and this is the room you will probably want to furnish first.

In most modern schemes, the living-room serves as a dining-room too, and the shape is usually small, square, or small, oblong, or small, square at one end with dining recess at the other. Take a good look at the space. It may look empty now, but at least it's spacious. As you begin furnishing, you will find that the room begins to shrink. It is good sense, artistically as well as financially, to limit yourself to a certain number of pieces of furniture. Many attractive rooms have been ruined by overcrowding, and it makes cleaning twice as awkward. If you are a working woman, you haven't time to clean oftener than once a week, so you should be able to streamline as far as possible.

It's a good idea to work out, first, the priorities for each room. In the living-room, the priorities are fabrics, furniture and flooring. Of these, I'd place fabrics—curtains, that is—at the top of the list. You can do without a carpet or rugs: you can sit on one orange box and eat off another. But you will want some privacy, and—especially if you move in mid-winter—the extra comfort and warmth that drawn curtains give. Naked windows can make a room look very bleak indeed.

The choice of fabrics can be bewildering, but because you are cost-conscious, it is wiser to forget about brocades, brocatelles and expensive tweed-type fabrics. Look for easy-care materials. Make sure they will wash, or at least take kindly to the coin-op dry cleaner's.

If you are lucky enough to have two windows in the living-room—and the square/oblong room I mentioned above often has a window at either end, making a pleasant through room—it is not necessary to use

Fig 4 Choosing fabrics: ask about wash and wear.

the same fabric for both windows. One large firm has an exciting range of
flowered cottons with matching repps, and this can look very attractive.
But you don't have to choose an expensive fabric. You could carry out
your own matching with a flowered cotton from a chain store
at under £1 a yard, pick out a colour from the pattern and use a plain
repp or cotton in this shade for the other window.

Remember that you will be using the room all the year round and it is
unlikely that you can afford two sets of curtains, so you must choose a

fabric that will look good at any season. Heavy velvet curtains look
splendid in winter, but would you want to live with them on a hot July
day? When you are searching for fabrics forget the old idea about heavy
curtains being essential for winter warmth. If your home is a modern
one, it is more than likely that you will have some form of central heating
or storage radiators, so you don't need thick curtains. Or if you have open
fires, thick curtains will become easily soiled and will have to be cleaned
fairly often. Lightweight curtains have to be cleaned too, but they are
easier to wash.

So for curtain material you could choose a printed cotton, linen or a
cotton repp. Repp is an excellent choice for a first home. You can buy it at
under £1 a yard. It is tough, hard-wearing, and washes beautifully,
and comes in a range of attractive colours.

Hessian is inexpensive too, and you can buy it in many beautiful colours.
It costs under 60p a yard, and is sold in widths of 50in so it makes
economical curtaining material. But it is important that hessian curtains
should be lined, and it is better to dry-clean rather than wash, so you
should add this into the cost.

If you already own some old curtains—perhaps cushion covers too—
which look a little tired, you can give them a completely new lease of life
by dyeing. There isn't room here to go into the instructions, but there
are excellent leaflets giving the fullest information, available from the
leading dye manufacturers. (*See* Where to find out about . . . p. 99.)
These leaflets give lots of guidance on how to dye everything from
curtains and towels to carpets. You can also find plenty of help on tie-
dyeing. With tough white cotton, twisted and coiled, or knotted and
pleated, you could produce your own unusual designs, and make sure of
getting exactly the colour you want. For material you could use
unbleached cotton or white cotton huck, which you can buy in most
stores or through mail order at under 40p a yard.

If your home has large picture windows, you may have to buy net
curtains too. Most stores have a large display of all sorts of nets. The
choice can be rather bewildering, but it is helpful to remember that
terylene net is the best choice because it is not affected by sunlight.

Remember too, that if you have patterned curtains, a patterned net can look very fussy, and it is better to choose something simple and plain. Because this is a guide to a home on a budget, you may have to turn away from the beautiful Scandinavian nets and look at the budget counter or remnant stand. Among the remnants you may pick up a bargain because you can sometimes find a cut length that exactly fits your window. Remember that nets shrink, so allow for this (see the table at the end of the book, p. 93, for yardages required). Don't worry if your remnant of net looks rather grubby. A soak in hot water and detergent will soon bring it back to life. Look too, for special offers at sale times, since stores will often sell bargains of net in the broader widths.

Sales shopping for materials can result in some good bargains, but it is always important not to let economy go to your head. You may find some very cheap material which seems like a wonderful bargain, but it is always best to stop and ask yourself, 'will it wash?', 'will it wear?', and 'do I really like the colour/pattern?' And if you are buying curtain fabric in the sales, do check how much it will cost in all, including lining. If you're buying a remnant, make sure that there is enough material in the remnant for your purpose. Before you shop, it's wise to write down exactly what you want, colour, fabric and measurements, so that you aren't tempted by anything that 'might just do'.

And as a general rule, when you are shopping for fabrics, it's best to ask the assistant for a piece of the fabric, so that you can take it home and get some idea how it will look in your room. If you live in a city which has a design centre or a showroom with room sets, you can often see how a particular fabric will look when it is made up and hung.

Then you will need furniture. Your basic needs are a table and chairs (armchairs and dining chairs). If you are furnishing on the minimum you may not be able to afford new furniture—for example, most modern tables begin at a basic price around £30, and that's a big item in anyone's budget.

So don't disregard the secondhand shop. The Consumer Association publishes an excellent guide called *Buying Secondhand* (75p), which includes advice on buying furniture at secondhand shops, at auctions, through the secondhand departments of large stores, through Salvation Army depots, and other sources. You can order this booklet direct from the Consumer Association (address on p. 102), or the reference department of your local library will probably have a copy.

It helps to look round your neighbourhood and find a good secondhand dealer. Tell him just what you want, and he will look out for a suitable piece of furniture for you. For example, in my local shop I found a good, oval gate-legged table, for just £9. Its shape balances the squareness of the room and the surface polishes up beautifully.

When you are buying secondhand furniture, it is important to make sure that the legs of tables and chairs are strong enough. Lean on the table before you buy and sit in the chairs. It is wise to avoid secondhand shopping late in the day, when you are tired. For one thing, you will probably rush into a purchase without looking critically at the item (this applies to all shopping, of course). For another thing, when you are tired, *any* chair feels comfortable, as long as you can rest your weary feet, and it isn't until you get home that you find the chair isn't quite as well-sprung as you had expected.

Dining chairs are harder to find secondhand than tables, for they are much in demand. Also dealers are usually unwilling, understandably, to split a set, and you may find yourself with six dining chairs when you only wanted three. But you may be lucky enough to find a couple of solid chairs with strong frames. Don't worry if these have hideous 1930-type rexine seats. It is easy enough (see p. 23) to remove the seats and recover.

In most secondhand shops there are plenty of cheap bentwood chairs often painted in dull browns, and unpromising at first sight. But these are a good buy because this wood can be stripped and varnished and painted to suit your own colour scheme. Stripping and repainting chairs is a very satisfying occupation but it does need time and patience.

Scrub the chairs thoroughly first and look out for woodworm holes. A good dealer won't sell you anything badly wormed, but you may find the odd small hole, showing that woodworm has been there at some time or another. Old woodworm holes are neat round holes. New woodworm holes look just the same, but you can tell that the woodworm is still there because of the powdery substance that falls out of the holes. No need to despair, though. You can buy a good proprietary liquid, marketed as Rentokil, which will dispose of woodworm and prevent its return.

RENEWING OLD CHAIRS

*Fig 5 Paint the chair with stripper. Gloves and glasses will protect
you against splashes.*

This liquid comes in a can with a nozzle attachment and you just inject
the liquid into the holes and leave it to dry.

I like to wash furniture with washing soda too. Use plenty of soda
in really hot water and scrub thoroughly, then put the piece of
furniture outside in the fresh air to dry, if you can.

Now paint on the paint stripper, using a large brush and working well into
the corners. Leave this on for about 10–15 minutes, then the old paint will
become soft, and you can easily scrape it off. It is a good idea to
wear gloves and glasses while doing this, and of course mop up any

Fig 6   Remove softened paint.

splashes right away as the stripper is acid and can burn. You may need a
scrubbing brush and a small brush (an old toothbrush will do) to get
right into the corners. When you have removed all the old paint, scrub
well again and rub down the wood with glasspaper.

Now you are ready to paint or varnish. Polyurethane gloss paints are a
godsend to the home decorator because they produce such a professional
finish. You can use a colour or one of the wood stains. These usually
come in pint-size tins and the pint size is more than enough for two
dining chairs. You will need a varnish too. Buy the varnish in the same
brand as the stain. Semi-gloss is best for furniture, as the very high gloss
can become too glaring.

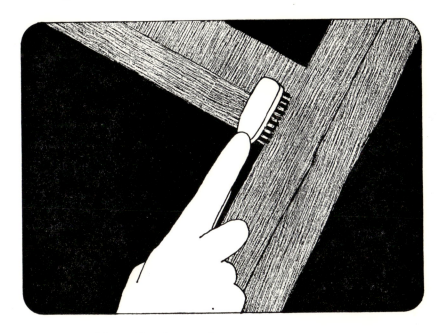

Fig 7   Use an old toothbrush to get into corners.

A friend in the decorating trade gave me the following helpful tips about staining, and they really do produce excellent results.

Apply the stain with an ordinary paint brush, then take an old rag and work the stain into the wood, smoothing it along the grain of the wood and rubbing it in. This gives a beautifully smooth effect. Then leave it to dry—for twenty-four hours if you can. If the stain is too light, give it another coat, and leave it for a further twenty-four hours. (I did say it took time and patience!) Finally, when the coat of stain is quite dry, paint on the clear varnish. Work smoothly, and watch out for drips because they show on the finished surface.

If you are really serious about refurbishing old chairs it is worth while attending an evening class to learn how to do it properly. You can of course learn to cover chairs with webbing or foam rubber by yourself, but the advantage of classes is that you learn, for a small outlay, to do it the correct way, and you also have the use of the proper tools, which are expensive to buy.

Fig 8   Rub with glasspaper when the chair is quite dry.

Fig 9   Smooth the stain along the grain of the wood.

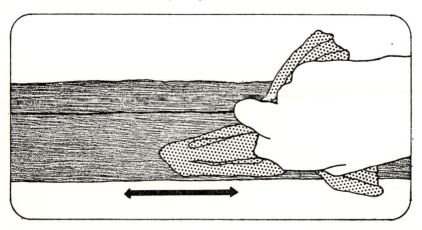

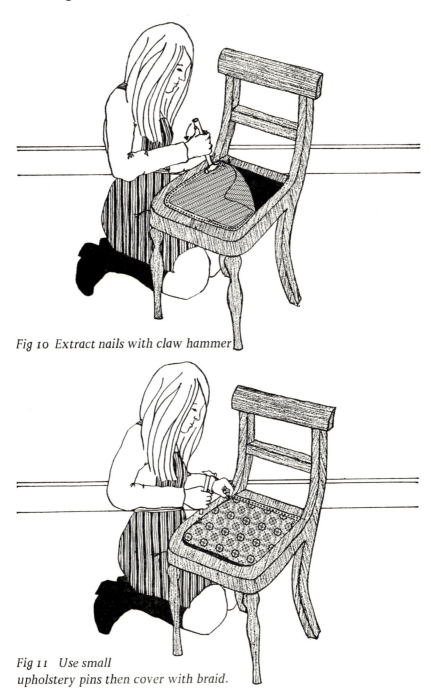

Fig 10 Extract nails with claw hammer

Fig 11 Use small upholstery pins then cover with braid.

The amateur working at home can, however, make a competent job of
replacing old drop-in seats on dining chairs.

It is reasonably easy too, to remove and replace old upholstery on a chair
of simple design. It is not a good idea to cover the old upholstery. That
way, you won't get a perfect fit. It is much better to remove the old
permanent cover, using claw hammer and screwdriver and stripping off
any old braid. You can then measure the seat cover. It is a good idea
at this stage to make a paper pattern based on the old seat cover. Pin the
paper pattern on to the chair, working from back to front, then transfer
the pattern to the fabric. Do not forget to allow for turnings and tuck-in.
The fabric can then be tacked to the frame with upholstery tacks. It is
important to get the fabric stretched tight before you tack finally,
and glue down at the corners, using an all-purpose adhesive and mitring
the corners neatly.

Latex or plastic foam is a splendid aid to the do-it-yourself furnisher.
Seating is quite a problem when you are hard up and one answer is to
make large comfortable floor cushions, using Latex or plastic foam as a
base. You can buy large squares of Latex about 18in square, at just over
£1. Covered with a cheap repp, hessian or flowered cotton, these squares
would make inexpensive extra seats if you like curling up on the floor.
Three together would make a ground level settee or an emergency bed
base. If you want added height you could put three cushions, one on
top of the other. They are not sold in sizes deeper than 4in deep, so you
would need to put three together to get a good-sized pouffee of 12in deep.

If you are shopping secondhand it is worth trying to find a small
chesterfield. These sofas are rather difficult to find, because they are just
the right size for the small home. Unless you are expert, it is best to have
a sofa re-covered professionally, and be sure to get quotations first, or
you may find that your bargain is not such a bargain after all. To
re-cover a small sofa you will need about 4 yds of 48in-wide material,
and here it is well worth keeping an eye on the remnant counters, where
you can often find an end-of-roll remnant being sold more cheaply.
Corduroy, brocatelle or heavy tweed are all good choices for upholstery.
Repp is not so good because it tends to stretch and wrinkle.

You may decide that you can get good value for your money by buying
at auction sales. In some parts of the country you can still find splendid

bargains at country house sales. But at the ordinary town sale, you will often discover that the dealers have arrived first, and you can easily be carried away by the wonderful bargain of the chairs that no one seems to want. It is only when you bring the chairs home that you find the springs are broken or that the seats are bug-infested. And of course if there was a viewing day beforehand, and there always is, you cannot claim. It is usually better to buy through a dealer, whose judgement you can trust, rather than risk a hasty and ill-considered buy.

And finally, if you buy a new armchair, do take time to compare prices. Sit in the chair and make sure that it is well sprung and gives enough back support. Light-coloured upholstery fabrics can look fine in the shop but can soon become grubby in the home, so make sure before you buy that the fabric can be cleaned easily or the covers removed altogether for cleaning.

And now, flooring. If your home is a modern one with wood or parquet flooring, you may decide that, to begin with anyway, it is cheaper to polish regularly and use rugs to cover the floor than spend a lot on a carpet immediately. Before you move in, take a good look at the floor. A wood floor in poor condition can be improved by sanding, but this is a job you ought to carry out before you furnish.

Sanding a floor isn't difficult, and with a very little practice you can produce most professional results. If you live near a large town, you can probably hire a sanding machine by the day from one of the large hire firms. You pay for the hire of the machine, the cartage (unless you collect and return it yourself), the glasspaper you use and any damage to the machine.

Make sure that you find out from the hire firm exactly how to operate the type of machine you hire, and especially how to insert the glasspaper round the drum. This can take a little practice, and you will waste quite a number of sheets of paper if you don't do it properly.

Clear the room before you begin. Most sanding machines are fitted with vacuum bags, so there isn't anything like the dust that there used to be with old-fashioned sanding machines, but there is still a little dust, and it is best to sweep or vacuum as you go along.

C

Fig 12 *Sanding old or worn floorboards. These sanding machines can be hired for the day.*

Another thing. It is a good idea to warn the neighbours that you are going to be sanding a floor. This machine creates a great deal of noise, and can disturb other people—especially in a block of flats.

To operate the machine, you simply switch on and guide the machine along, rather like a vacuum cleaner. Before switching on, the machine should be slightly tilted upwards, then the front gently lowered on to the floor. Don't be tempted to do too large an area at once. It is better to cover a few square feet successfully than have to re-sand a patch. Old floor should have the nails punched down before you begin.

With any such machine, you must be careful how you handle it. Don't tamper with the machine while it is switched on, and make sure that the main switch and the switch on the machine are off before you attempt to change the paper on the drum.

Once you have sanded the floor down to the bare wood, clean it with white spirit and allow to dry before you begin to apply seal. You can buy a number of good proprietary seals and these are applied in two coats. The first is applied sparingly with a cloth and allowed to dry for about six hours. The second coat is usually painted on with a brush. Here it is best to cover only a small square at a time so that you are sure to cover the floor evenly. The second coat will take about twenty-four hours to dry and won't be completely hard for about a week. Whatever type of seal you use, remember to read the directions carefully for professional results.

It costs about £3 a day to hire a sanding machine, plus extra for seal, cartage and paper. Prices may vary from one district to another, so it is best to obtain quotations from several firms if you can.

If there are only small discoloured patches on your wood floor, you may not think it worth the trouble and expense of sanding the whole floor. In this case you can good results with steel wool and elbow grease, polishing with a circular movement a small area at a time. When the surface dirt is removed, you can then seal and polish.

An easy way to keep a wood floor in good condition is to use one of the non-slip polishes for a thorough first clean, and then polish at intervals with an impregnated mop.

Rugs add a look of comfort and are reasonably cheap, and they can be taken up for cleaning. Rush matting is attractive too. You can buy this by the square yard, which works out cheaper than buying rush mats, or if you wish you can buy oval or circular mats for a particular area. Another advantage of rush matting is that it is quite easy to clean. You can vacuum it, scrub and beat it, and it looks good with most furnishing schemes.

You can also buy reasonably cheap cotton rugs in bright colours and if you want to cover a sitting area, two or three of these can be sewn together to make a large rug. Sew loosely so that the rugs can be unpicked for washing.

If you decide that a carpet is going to be a good investment, it is worth while taking time to shop around the stores, keep an eye on the discount warehouses, and find out as much as you can from the advisory organisations such as the British Carpet Centre (see address on p. 100), which offers a number of very helpful leaflets, and will advise by post if you can't visit their London headquarters.

Because a carpet is an expensive buy, you want to be sure that you get good value for your money. You must consider before you buy just how much heavy wear the carpet will receive. It is false economy to buy a cheap, light-weight carpet for a living area which has to take a lot of treading. And don't forget to include in your budget enough to buy an underlay too. Felt and rubber is best for the underlay and it is not economical to try to make do with old newspapers spread out across the floor. A good underlay will prolong the life of the carpet.

If you are economising, a carpet square would probably be your best buy. In some warehouses you can find these squares at a cheaper rate, because they are off-cuts from larger orders. The advantage of a square is that you can turn it round when it gets worn in one particular place. In a room with a dining recess and a sitting area, you could use a carpet square for the sitting area, and rugs for the dining recess where a carpet wouldn't be so necessary.

Another good choice for budget flooring is haircord. There are various types of haircord at prices which are around £1·50 to £2·10 for a square yard, so that it is much cheaper to use this if you want to have a fitted carpet throughout a room. Although it obviously does not have the warmth of carpeting, haircord is strong and hard-wearing, and is produced in so many attractive colours that it does give a room a furnished look immediately.

And that basically, is all you need for a living-room. The extras—bookcase, lamps, storage units and pictures—are things which can be added as you go along. These items can add lots of personality and don't cost much either. (See chapter 9.)

4 THE BEDROOM

Furnishing a bedroom right from the beginning need not be a problem—nor need the room become a sort of junk room for unwanted pieces of furniture. Right from the start, you can plan wisely and inexpensively to make an attractive room.

The vital needs in a bedroom are a bed and enough storage space. When you think of the things you don't really need and can do without, the list grows longer. You don't really need an old-fashioned wardrobe (they are usually far too big for modern homes anyway). You don't need a dressing table—the usual type of dressing-table takes up far too much space and is tricky to manoeuvre into the right light. You don't need a bedside cabinet (the secondhand shops are full of them, which proves that other people have decided they can do without too). You don't need a carpet—at first, anyway. If you do decide that a carpet will add comfort, you can safely choose an inexpensive carpet or a haircord, because it won't get as much wear here as in the rest of the home.

So you need a bed, some storage space, a mirror, a small bedside table of some sort to hold books, alarm clock, etc., lamp, curtains and bedding.

Decide first whether you want your bedroom to be feminine or practical. If you decide on the feminine look, try to avoid the silk and satin type of furnishing. It dates, is expensive, looks fussy and the fabrics are awkward to clean.

Before you buy a bed, take a good look round the stores and don't let the salesman pressurise you into buying before you are certain of your choice. If he is a good salesman he won't want to sell you a particular make or type of bed. And anyway, it is you who must sleep on the bed. So do try the bed properly for size and comfort before you buy. And don't disregard the bed that is reduced in the sales. It may be reduced only because there is a chip off the wood, or perhaps that particular line is old stock. And of course, it is foolish to limit your choice just because you don't like the particular floral pattern of the mattress covering. You will see the base of the bed only when you strip and make the bed, so it doesn't matter in the least what it looks like.

It is worth paying a little extra for a headboard if you have a light paper in the bedroom, and are worried by the idea of marks on the wall behind the bed.

When it comes to storage space, you may be lucky, and have built-in cupboards, in which case your problem is solved for you. Even if you have built-in cupboards, it is still worth while taking a good look at the hanging space inside. If the rails aren't at the correct height for you, or if they won't take the width of hanging coats then remove the rails and have them replaced at a suitable height. Remember that you are going to be living here for some time, and it is a good deal easier to make alterations like this at an early stage.

Try to save as much space as you can in these cupboards. In a long, narrow cupboard it is no use putting rails horizontally across the cupboard because the item you want will always be right at the very back. Better to fix a rail lengthways. You can have it fixed to the wall with brackets, far enough away from the wall to allow clothes to hang without touching the wall. This way you will still have space underneath for shoes and boxes and a considerable amount of walk-in space still left in the cupboard.

But if you don't have fitted cupboards, one of the cheapest alternatives is whitewood funiture. Whitewood cupboards and wardrobes vary in price, so it is a good idea to shop around and get hold of the catalogues of various firms. At sale time, you may find cupboards reduced in price because they have been slightly battered—or if you notice a piece of whitewood that is chipped, the salesman may knock something off the cost for you. And of course, it doesn't matter if the wood is slightly chipped. You can easily glasspaper any battered edges, and the whole piece will be sized and painted anyway, so a small chip will not be noticed.

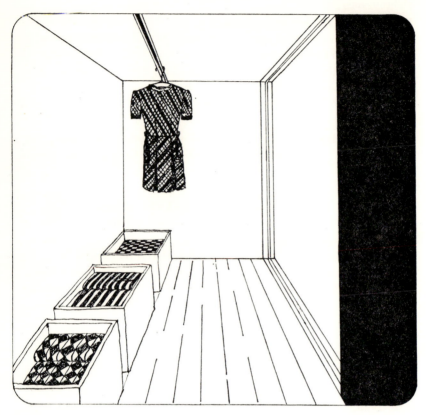

Fig 13 One way of using space inside a walk-in cupboard.

When painting whitewood, do allow plenty of time for the various coats
of primer and paint to dry. First of all, give the piece of furniture a good
coat of primer. You can buy suitable primer for whitewood in any do-
it-yourself shop. Then you want to give it at least two coats of gloss paint.
The new polyurethane paints are extremely useful to the home decorator
because they don't drip, and you can produce a smooth coat without
any streaks. Be sure to allow plenty of time between coats, however,
so that the first coat is quite dry before you attempt the second.

If you want to make a whitewood cupboard look out of the ordinary
you can fit glass or brass handles, and pick out the panels in contrasting
colour or even use wallpaper remnants to cover the panels.

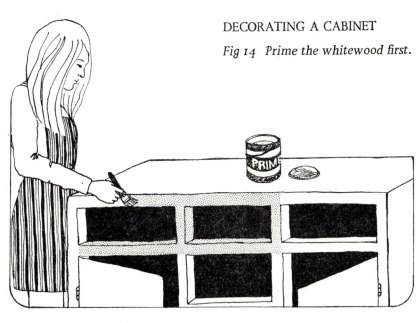

DECORATING A CABINET

Fig 14 Prime the whitewood first.

Fig 15 Follow with two coats of gloss paint.

Fig 16   Decorate panels in a contrasting colour...

Fig 17   ...or with pieces of left-over wallpaper.

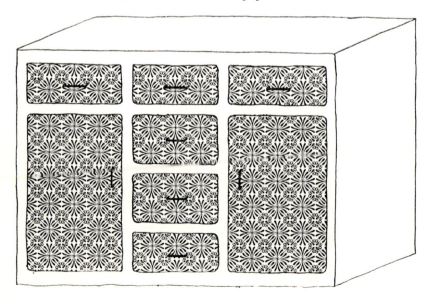

What about a mirror and dressing-table substitute? If you are very hard up, a mirror and dressing table can be expensive items. You can make do with a small chest of drawers. You can find these in secondhand shops, though there is a great demand for them and what you are most likely to find is the dreary institutional-type chest, painted chocolate brown. Make sure that it is free from woodworm; scrub with washing soda as described in the last chapter, and leave the chest out in the open air to get rid of any musty smell, before you strip the old paint and begin priming and painting. Remember, if you are buying a chest, to pull out the drawers to see that they run smoothly. You can't expect the drawers of the secondhand chest to run as smoothly and silkily as those of the craftsman-made antique, but they should be free from knots. If the drawers do stick, a candle rubbed over the edge of the wood will usually help.

A mirror can be fixed to the wall above the chest. Often in specialist shops you can obtain pieces of mirror glass cut to size, and this can be cheaper than buying a ready-made mirror. This makes a perfectly adequate substitute for a dressing-table, and if you need a long mirror, it can be fixed to the inside of a cupboard door or of a small wardrobe cupboard.

You will also need some kind of bedside table to hold lamp, alarm clock, books, etc. Most bedside cabinets sold as such don't seem to have nearly enough space for all these items, and fixing a shelf above the bed, which seems a good idea on the surface, is often rather unpractical. Either it is too high to reach from the bed, or too low, in which case you bump your head as you leap up to stop the alarm clock ringing. It is better to fix a shelf to the wall slightly to one side of the bed but still near enough to reach.

Or you could find a small table about the same height as the bed—either whitewood or secondhand—which would serve as a coffee table in the living-room too. A whitewood table could either be painted or covered with adhesive laminated plastic. The type of table often sold as a telephone table can be useful too.

When it comes to choosing bedding, this can prove expensive. It may be that you have moved from a furnished flat where linen was supplied, and in this case, sheets, blankets and bedspreads can make a sizeable hole in your budget. If you have a sewing machine you can make your own

sheets and bedspreads for a good deal less than the price of those you
buy in the shops. Some wholesale and mail order firms sell sheeting
by the yard and this comes in such an attractive range of colours that
you can match your bedlinen to the rest of the colour scheme. This
sheeting is available in all shades from coffee and dark blue to yellow and
deep cherry red and cool stripes of lilac and pale green. A scheme of
dark blue and turquoise sheets, matched to a pale grey and white room,
would be a good colour scheme. The sheeting sells in widths of 70in and
90in and you need about 5½ to 6 yards for each pair of sheets—70in
is of course the size for a single bed, 90in for a double. At under 60p a yard
for 70in wide material in plain colours, this means that you can make a
pair of single bed sheets for about £3.60. (More where to buy details
on p. 99.)

All you need to do is turn and machine the hems at either end. Allow
a 2in hem at the bottom and about 4–5in at the top. If you want to add a
finishing touch, you can trim the sheets. For example, a couple of yards
of broderie anglaise, stitched under the top hem so that the edging
is just showing, makes an expensive-looking finish to pastel-coloured
sheets. Broderie anglaise always looks fresh and attractive, but you can
use any kind of trimming as long as it will stand up to frequent washing.

You can also buy candlewick by the yard—this is tough and hard-wearing,
and warm enough so that you don't need a quilt on top.

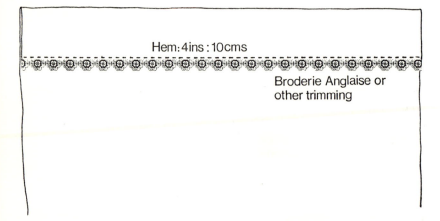

Hem: 4ins : 10cms

Broderie Anglaise or
other trimming

Fig 18 Home-made sheets with a 4-in hem and washable trimming.

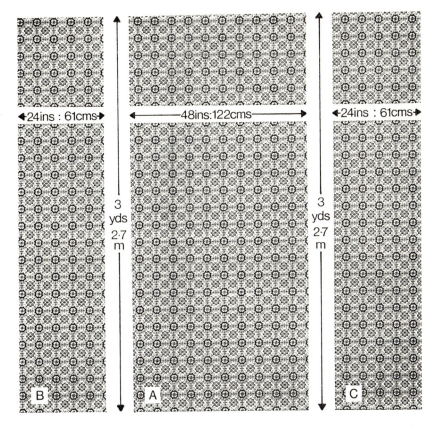

◄24ins : 61cms►   ◄────────48ins:122cms────────►   ◄24ins : 61cms►

3 yds 2·7 m   3 yds 2·7 m

B   A   C

*Fig 19 Cutting out a simple bedspread. Join B to A and A to C right
sides together.*

Cotton lace bedspreads are pretty and practical and keep their
crispness, especially if you add starch when finishing the laundering, or
iron when slightly damp. You can make these for yourself. If you shop
around the furnishing department of any large store, you will find that
you can buy cotton lace, usually used for curtains, under 60p a yard,
usually 48in wide. You will need about 6 yards, which means that you can
make a single bed size spread for about £3.60. You can also buy 70in
widths and if you are making a spread for a single bed, then the
spread will be the same width as a sheet and you don't need to cut it. In
this case you will require about 3 yards.

If you are using the 48in wide material, it is important to make sure that you get the pattern of the lace right in the centre. Cut the first 3 yards to make the middle panel of the spread. Then divide the remaining 3 yards into two strips, each 24in wide, to make the side panels. All you need to do is make sure that the side panels which are each 24in wide, match the pattern of the centre panel, before you begin stitching.

It is a good idea to add a coloured sheet under the lace spread to match your colour scheme. One of the most attractive bedrooms I've seen had a white cotton lace spread over a vivid yellow sheet to match the sunny yellow of the curtains.

Another good, cheap fabric to use in a bedroom is mattress ticking. This is not only cheap—you can buy it at around 65p a yard—but it is sold in widths of 56in which means that you will require less of it than you would of a material which is 48in wide. For a very modern bedroom, you could use black and white mattress ticking for the curtains (it is strong and thick, so you wouldn't need to line them), a plain white combed cotton or a scarlet bedspread, and sheets and cushions in bright orange or scarlet.

And don't forget that a really colourful blanket can double as a bedspread, and save the cost of blankets too.

You probably won't need a quilt in a modern, well-heated home. If you are economising on linen, one of the continental down quilts would, for an initial outlay, save you buying any blankets at all. They are quite expensive to buy, but you could save money by making your own covers.

You will also need a bedroom chair of some kind. The white-painted bentwood chair is useful here, but if you want a piece of furniture which can happily move between bedroom and living-room, then look out for white willow. A basket chair costs about £6, and for around £13 you can buy a settee.

And that is basically all you need for a bedroom. Of course you will add more items as you can afford them, but the bedroom is one room where a clever arrangement of furniture, clean, cool colours and a good choice of pictures and extras will pay more dividends than investing in expensive items of furniture. It is worth remembering too, that your tastes may

change, and in a year or two you may have more money to spend
and it is much easier and less expensive to re-style a bedroom than any
other room. For one thing, bedrooms in modern homes are usually fairly
small, and this is one room where re-papering and painting won't involve
a vast outlay of money.

5 THE HALL AND ENTRANCE

In a modern home you will be very lucky to have a hall at all. Nothing baronial about the 12 × 3ft passage that advertisements call 'entrance hall'. None of the mistletoe bough atmosphere about the tiny space cluttered with umbrellas, shoes and everything you discard on the way in. But because it is so small, the hall does give you lots of scope and the opportunity to try out experimental ideas.

It's here that you can carry out your ideas for way-out colours because you don't have to live with them at close quarters. You simply pass through the hall and the sizzling orange that might become a little trying in your bedroom will be warm and welcoming in the hall.

The first rule is: 'Don't spend a lot of money on expensive paper or carpet for a hall.' This is one part of the house which will get a fair amount of wear. It isn't very welcoming to glare at your guests when they lean against the costly paper or tramp in muddy shoes over the best carpet. By the nature of things, too, this will be the last part of the house to be decorated, so you won't *have* a great deal of money to spend.

Look back for a minute to your plans for furnishing colours. I think it is a good idea to marry the colours of your front door to the inner hall scheme. For example, if you have a pale grey front door, you could have a dark blue and white scheme for the hall. A dark olive green front door could be complemented by a raspberry and olive scheme inside. A yellow front door could have a yellow flowered paper and door curtains inside. You don't really need carpeting in the hall, but if it looks too stark without, you could use a haircord, or an inexpensive washable cotton rug, or one of those very cheap Indian mats which wash quite well and come in a range of attractive soft coloured patterns. Look out too for carpet samples. You can often find odd samples (perhaps a yard of a good Wilton) for about £2, which will make an ideal mat for the hall.

If you have room it is a good idea to have some sort of shelving in the hall to hold the odds and ends that you may need beside the telephone, or which can be used to display plates and plants. You can buy shelves in whitewood to paint, or you could use orange boxes which would double as a seat beside a telephone. Rub the boxes down with glasspaper first, paint with size (several coats), and then use gloss paint or varnish.

It is also a good idea to have something to hold umbrellas. Any circular container about 1ft high would do. You can cover it with adhesive laminated plastic, and add lampshade trimming round the top if you have the time and energy to spare.

You also need somewhere to hang coats and you can either buy a rack to fix to the wall (we come to the fixing in a moment), or use individual hooks which you can buy from any chain store.

Drilling holes is not difficult. It helps, of course, if you have a friend with an electric drill, but you can do it yourself with a hand drill, and a set of Rawlplugs.

RAWLPLUGGING

Fig 20 Measure the screw thread against the plug.

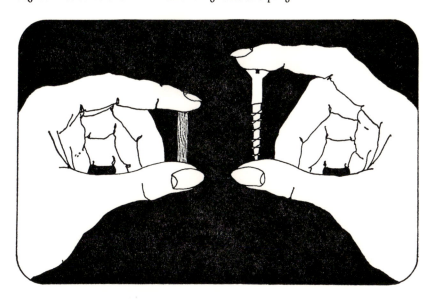

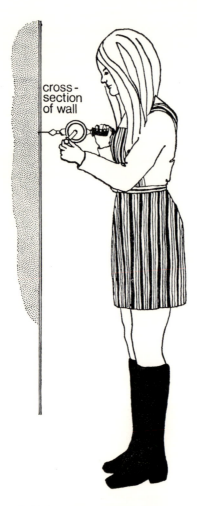

cross-
section
of wall

Fig 21   Remember to drill the hole at right angles.

You can save a lot of time and temper when drilling if you remember to hold the drill straight, at right angles to the wall, and drill directly into the wall. This may sound very elementary but it is so easy to start with drill slightly on the slant and you will never get a clean hole.

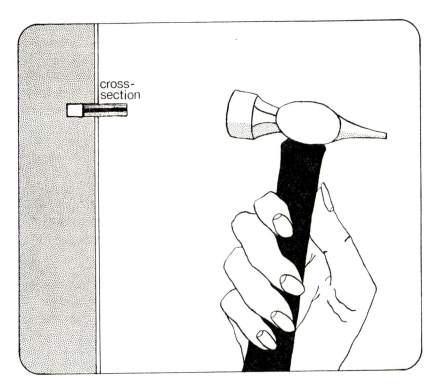

cross-
section

Fig 22 Tap the plug into the hole with a hammer.

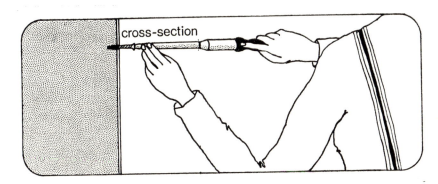

cross-section

Fig 23 Fit the screw into the plug.

Make sure that the hole is quite clear before you insert the Rawlplug—
blowing into it is the best way. Then push the Rawlplug into the hole. At
your first attempt you may have to tap the Rawlplug lightly with a
hammer to get it to go in, but don't hit too hard or you will, obviously,
damage the plaster on the wall. If the plug is too small for the hole, don't
try to pack the surround with Polyfilla or any such material. Extract
the plug and try a larger size. It is best to start by selecting a Rawlplug
of the same length as the threaded part of the screw you are going to
use. Once the Rawlplug is quite firmly set into the hole, insert the screw
and keep on turning the screwdriver until the screw grips and doesn't
fall out of the hole. This is much the best and tidiest way of fixing screws
into a wall and they do look much neater than a nail simply hammered
into the wall with lots of plaster flaking about. It takes a little time to
become expert and it is best to practise your first attempts on a piece of
wall where they won't be too obvious.

Pictures in the hall can be posters, pieces of wallpaper, book jackets—see
the chapter on extras, chapter 9. Anything ephemeral will do because
you can always take down vivid prints and posters when you become
tired of them.

It isn't worth while spending a great deal of money on the hall, but do try
to allow enough to have proper locks put on your front door. It is money
well spent to invest a few pounds in a proper mortice lock. A Yale
lock on its own is an invitation to burglars. And if you live alone, and
are nervous, a chain on the door or an inside bolt will give you an extra
sense of security.

Door curtains are a good idea when you have a little cash to spare. If
you have a glass front door, they add a look of comfort and help to keep
the heat from escaping.

6　THE KITCHEN

Even if this is your first home, you have probably lived in rented accommodation for a time, and you will own some crockery, cutlery and such oddments as saucepans, tea towels and a few gadgets. In a kitchen you can usually get by with the minimum. You could, if you wanted, cook with one saucepan only. So let's reckon what the essentials are. A cooker, a refrigerator (absolutely essential for the working woman who can only shop once a week), and storage space.

Design first. It is most unlikely that you can plan your kitchen from scratch and the alluring pictures in the glossy magazines will have to remain a distant dream as far as you are concerned. But if you are moving into a modern house, then you will find that most builders are fairly enlightened about the fitments they include and you are not likely to discover a fitted refrigerator in the darkest part of the kitchen. Still, there is a great deal you can do yourself to make the room more habitable. In a modern development the kitchens will be identical boxes, but take a look at your neighbours' kitchens and you will find that every one has been adapted differently by the owner.

Where to put the cooker and refrigerator is not likely to be your particular problem. But if you have a choice, remember that it is most important that the sink and cooker should be on the same stretch of wall and facing the light. How often do you see pictures of modern kitchens that have the sink unit facing a blank wall? Of course, this is a matter of personal taste, but if you are a working woman you will be using the sink on dark mornings and late in the day, and you want to have as much light as possible on your work. Many modern designers tend to put the sink against a side wall, away from the window, and I have read an argument that this is a reasonable plan because women nowadays don't spend as much time at the sink as they used to. I think the writer was wrong. Most women would tell you that any time spent at the sink is tedious, and a pleasant outlook, or any outlook at all, is necessary.

Fig 24 A simple and efficient kitchen layout.

Then working surfaces. If the surface isn't fixed already, you can do a certain amount of planning. Make sure that your working surface, that is, the area where you will roll out pastry, squeeze oranges, prepare meat and so on, is near the sink and near the cooker. Make sure that it is at a suitable height and that the surface is level. This may seem obvious, but you would be surprised how many work surfaces slant, so that the water runs off and eggs roll on to the floor

You can buy ready-made units, have them built or construct your own from a kit. Because the price of ready-made units or kits is probably beyond you at the moment, it is worth calling in a carpenter, and having the work surface built where you want it at the correct height. This way, you can have as many shelves under the working top as you like. A cutlery drawer is essential but it is not necessary or practical to have too many drawers in the unit. They are very difficult to keep clean, and collect crumbs and dust in the corners. Also it is difficult to keep things tidy because you can never see just where they have got to. Remember, you will have a lot of large equipment to store, and it is much better to have a number of useful shelves under the unit, rather than a lot of drawers into which you can't see properly. Shelves mean too, that pots and pans and casseroles can be neatly stored away.

Before you have any cupboards built, it is a good plan to sit down and work out exactly what you want to store. You may not eat many vegetables, so you won't need a vegetable rack. You may want extra large and accessible shelves to store a mixer and blender. You may be a keen winemaker in which case you will need enough storage space to take your equipment and space to store the bottles.

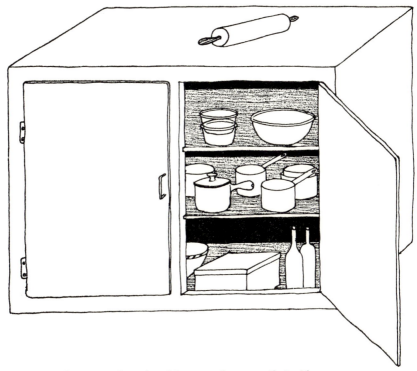

Fig 25 A home-made unit with space for utensils inside.

But how do you set about finding a carpenter? The little man around the corner who will come and build your units for next to nothing is a rare bird indeed in the 1970s. But there are ways to find a good carpenter. One of the ways is by a personal recommendation. Ask your neighbours or ask at the local newsagent's and they may be able to recommend someone.

The other way is by looking in the classified pages of a local trade directory. This is often quite a satisfactory way to go about it. For one thing, no one is likely to go to the trouble of advertising unless he is fairly business-like. You can, of course, look at the advertisements in the newsagent's window, but remember that the newsagent is not bound to act as a referee and can give no guarantee of the carpenter's standards.

One thing you should not do is to give the job to the man who calls at the door offering handyman services. For a start, he may not be a genuine handyman. He may simply be 'casing the joint' and casting a professional eye over such valuables as you may have, so that he may return at a later date. Or he may persuade you into parting with money for wood and other materials, and that will be the last you see of him. Anyway, you should remember that if he were a really first-class carpenter, he wouldn't be touting round the doors for business. So do close the door firmly on the dubious doorstep handyman—he's so often out to make trouble for you and a dishonest living for himself.

So you've listed the number of possibles from the local directory. Now you ring them up and ask for a quotation. Don't forget about this stage. It's no use moaning about the cost when the carpenter has done the work. So you should get several estimates, but don't be tempted to choose the cheapest, just because it is the cheapest. You often have to pay for a good job well done, and the carpenter has to live too.

How do you know if he is a competent craftsman? One sure way is if he will take the trouble to come and look at the job to be done and advise you before giving a quotation. He should provide the wood and materials, but make sure that you know exactly what they will cost. Ask him too, how he would like to be paid. Some carpenters prefer you to pay in cash, to avoid bad debts and the trouble of sending out bills. But you should be sure that you get a receipt from him, with the word 'paid' and the date on it, and make sure that he signs it.

While most competent carpenters can knock up a cupboard without much difficulty, and you don't need to see the carpenter's union card to prove that he can do it, do be careful about employing spare-time electricians and plumbers. Especially with an electrician, find out if he is qualified before you employ him. It is often better to contact your local Electricity Board or to get a trained electrician to come along from a local shop.

Once your carpenter has built the units, you can save money by sizing them and painting them yourself. You need a couple of coats of primer. Leave them to dry before you begin painting with gloss paint, again two coats.

If you have a little more money to spend, you can buy ready-made whitewood cabinets and you will also need to prime and paint them yourself. The tops can be covered with long-lasting adhesive plastic. You can buy it cut to size, or buy it in sheets and cut it yourself with a sharp knife.

When buying such permanent fixtures as a cooker or a refrigerator, it is wise to shop around before you decide what to buy. Whether you decide on gas or electricity depends on your own preference, and also the types of fittings and plugs already in your home. If you are short of space a wall-hung refrigerator is a good idea (make sure that it is hung safely) or a small slim-line refrigerator. Most of these models hold quite a lot, even the small ones, and you don't really need a family-size refrigerator if you have only one or two in your family.

Flooring is not a great problem in the kitchen as most modern houses have good composition floors. If the floor is in good condition, there is no need to spend money on tiles, but you could put down sheet vinyl which is easy to lay, is quite cheap and can be taken up if you move house.

For hanging utensils, pegboard can be screwed onto the wall, and hooks can then be fixed into it to take ladle, fish slice, bacon scissors and other items which are in constant use.

Hardboard is another useful standby in the kitchen. You can use it—or laminated plastic—as a splash-back behind the cooker, or on any part of the wall which gets particularly dirty.

When decorating the kitchen, remember that you must use a paint or paper that can easily be washed down, because the kitchen walls will soon become spattered with grease spots from cooking. Unless you want a specially vividly patterned and colour paper, it is probably best to choose a fairly simple design or one colour of paint. In a tiny kitchen, and most kitchens in modern schemes are fairly minute, too 'busy' a wallpaper can get on your nerves.

And look out for the new non-drip gloss paints. These cover a surface in one coat and save all the tedious business of streaky surfaces and drip marks. They are ideal for kitchen use, as you will probably have quite a bit of woodwork to cover.

For the walls, emulsion or any paint that is easy to wash down should be used.

Since cleanliness is very important in the kitchen, cheap cotton curtains are probably best for your windows, as they are easy to launder. A roller blind looks attractive, but it ought to be of a washable material and easy to sponge down. Venetian blinds are practical only if you are conscientious about keeping them clean, since in a kitchen they will become much dirtier and greasier than you would expect.

Finally, safety. Even on the tightest budget safety should be your highest priority, remembering that a vast number of accidents take place in the home every year. Don't, in the interests of economy, skimp on proper checks on equipment. If you have central heating, make sure it is serviced regularly. Be sure, too, that all plugs and electrical equipment are checked for safety. A faulty lead on an electric kettle trailing through a puddle of water on the floor could be lethal. Keep an eye on all leads and cords and be sure they are replaced by a competent electrician as soon as they show signs of wear. Any loose plugs should be carefully tested and the same goes for any equipment that appears to be overheating.

And don't assume because fixtures look new that they are safe. Take a look at that cupboard—is it really safe, or is it hanging by a couple of screws? Check up now before it is too late.

7 THE BATHROOM

There is very little planning that need be done in a bathroom, because, like the hall, there isn't a lot of furniture needed. As long as the basic fittings are there, and the plumbing works satisfactorily, you can, to begin with, do without such extras as bath mat and laundry basket.

But because the bathroom is probably small, and you don't need to spend on furnishing, it is the ideal place to try out your decorating ideas. For example, if you have never papered a room before, it is not a bad idea to start with the bathroom and use an oil-based washable paper, rather than be discouraged by attempting to paper a large sitting-room. Once you become more experienced, you can go on to papering and painting larger areas. The next chapter tells you how to begin decorating.

But do remember, if you are painting the bathroom, to cover the bath properly before you begin. An old sheet, plus lots of newspapers, will do, but don't neglect this stage because it is very difficult indeed to get paint off a bath.

In the bathroom you can use cheap washable fabrics for curtains and accessories. A bright flowered cotton would be a good choice for curtains, and towelling by the yard is a useful aid for the budget-conscious home-maker. In the large stores you can buy self-coloured towelling for about 70p a yard.

It is 36in wide, so with two yards of towelling, you could make one bath towel 54 × 36in and one hand towel 36 × 18in, or you could make four hand towels. These are only suggestions, of course, and with a little ingenuity and some mathematical juggling, you could probably work out a much better way of using two yards. All you need to do is hem the ends, mitring the corners neatly, and this could be done either by hand or machine.

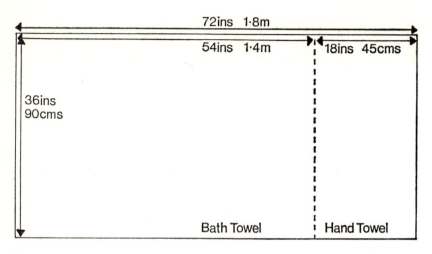

*Fig 26 How to use two yards of towelling to make a bath and hand
        towel.*

Offcuts of plastic foam are very useful, and if you have any left over
from making cushions, you could make sponges and other items. For
example, a piece of foam can be doubled over and seamed up two sides to
make a pocket. You fill this pocket with odd scraps of soap, then stitch
again. This makes a cheap sponge, and the soap fragments, being already
hard, last much longer.

To make a cabinet for storage, an orange box is ideal. Sand it down
first, giving it a good rub with the roughest grade of glasspaper. Then
give it a couple of coats of primer, allowing them to dry thoroughly
before painting with two coats of gloss paint, inside and outside. Unless
your box already has a division across the centre, you will have to make
a shelf of plywood across the middle or provide hooks inside. It you want
to keep the inside dust free, use a piece of cotton as a curtain across
the front (a piece of material with a casing at the top to take a length of
expanding curtain rod. Use two cup hooks at either side to take the
curtain.) This is an adults-only storage idea, though. If you have young
children in your household, you must have a proper medicine cabinet
with a lock. This is one area where it doesn't pay to skimp on cost.

It's very difficult to find glass jars that aren't expensive. But if you can pick up a few jars cheaply, they look attractive filled with small guest soaps or bath salts.

And of course the bathroom is the ideal place for growing indoor plants which like a humid atmosphere, and even, for raising from seed, outdoor plants that like damp moist conditions.

8 PAINT AND PAPER

Perhaps you have never painted before. It isn't difficult and you can obtain very satisfactory results with a little care and practice. And when you compare the cost of do-it-yourself with the charges of a professional decorator, you will be inspired to go ahead and try your hand at it.

First of all, you must prepare the walls for painting. This means that they should be clean and dry. To wash down the walls use a solution of sugar soap (cheap, from any hardware shop), or any proprietary brand of washing powder for floors and walls. Use warm water and a cloth or sponge, or a long-handled mop. Wash downwards, that is from top to bottom, so that you sweep the dirt down towards the floor. Use clean, cold water to rinse if need be, and leave to dry completely before painting.

Before you paint, you must fill in any cracks, using a cellulose filler such as Polyfilla, which you mix to a smooth paste with water. Remember that using this filler is rather like using icing sugar. You add the water very gradually, mixing liquid and filler together until the consistency is just right. Too much liquid will mean that the mixture is too soft and won't set properly. Too much Polyfilla will make the mixture crumbly and it won't spread smoothly when you apply it to the wall with a knife.

The makers recommend 2½ volumes of Polyfilla to one of water. And don't forget that the mixture sets very quickly so use it right away. For smaller jobs you can buy a cellulose filler in a plastic tube ready for use, so that you don't need to mix.

For painting, you will need paint (see chapter 12 for quantities) and brushes, plus turpentine, turps substitute, or any proprietary brand of cleaner for cleaning your brushes.

What kind of paint do you choose? It can be very bewildering if you are new to painting, but basically, you want emulsion for walls and gloss for

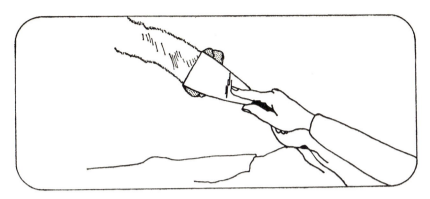

Fig 27 Using Polyfilla. It is important to smooth down the surface of the filler.

paintwork (that means walls, door, skirting board or any other wooden surface). You could also choose for walls one of the acrylic emulsions —these are sold under a number of trade names. They are good because they are more resistant to steam and condensation than ordinary emulsions and can be wiped down when they become grubby.

Do read the directions on the tin most carefully. A number of the new paints are very thick and need no stirring. If you stir, you will get an uneven streaky effect. Such paints are, however, very easy for the beginner to use and produce a smooth, even finish whether you have painted before or not.

For gloss painting, polyurethane gloss paint is very useful because it doesn't drip and you can paint the surface of a door or cupboard with one coat and avoid any of the unsightly drips that used to characterise amateur attempts at gloss painting.

Buy the best brushes you can afford and they will last for a very long time. You will need one medium-size brush and one for filling in the corners. You may find it easier to use a roller on the walls. You can buy this complete with tray from any do-it-yourself shop or chain store. The tray is filled with paint and the roller rolled gently back and forward in the tray until it is covered with paint (although it is a mistake to overload the roller, just as you should not overload the brush). Roll the roller up and down the wall and lightly across, covering only a small patch at a time. A roller does produce a very even, smooth effect and enables you to do the job quickly. Rollers should be used only with emulsion paint. You will not get satisfactory results with gloss.

Another useful item is a small tool like a set square, which is sometimes called a 'george'. This is used for painting round window frames so that you can achieve a neat painted edge without splashes on the glass.

And finally you need lots of old rags and newspapers to mop up the odd drips that there are bound to be—even with non-drip paints.

It is best to begin painting away from the light and work towards the window. Start at the top of the wall and work down. Paint in very narrow panels and strips. If you paint in too wide strips, you will find that you can see the join between one strip and the next.

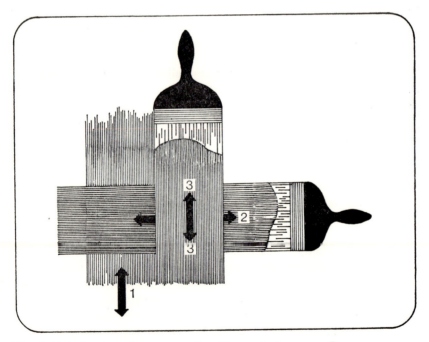

Fig 28 Painting in strips on a wall. 1. Down. 2. Across. 3. Down.

Never load a brush too heavily with paint, and try to use light strokes rather than a heavy pressure. The heavier emulsions and acrylic paints take a little time to dry, so don't worry if the paint looks slightly smudgy and streaky while it is still wet. Leave it to become quite dry. You may need to give the wall two coats of paint if you are painting on top of another colour, and it is very important that the first coat should be quite dry before you start the second.

When painting the skirting board you use gloss paint, of course, and work horizontally with light strokes. If you are using an ordinary gloss paint and not polyurethane paint, you will find that light strokes prevent streaking and dripping.

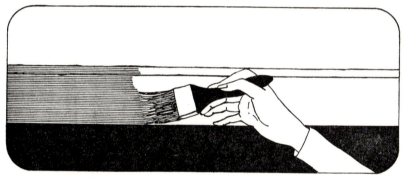

Fig 29   The right way to paint a skirting board, resting the little finger on the floor as a guide.

Painting a door is not difficult. If you have modern flush doors, it is simply a matter of starting at the top and painting in vertical strips until you reach the bottom. If yours is one of the old-fashioned panel doors, the best way is to begin with the centre panels, then paint the top, middle and bottom of the door horizontally, then paint vertically down the sides.

Again, it is very important not to overload the brush and to use quick, light strokes. If you have what professionals call 'a wet edge', that is a hard line vertically showing where the wet edge of the last strip has ended, you can avoid this looking too obvious on the finished wall by 'feathering'. This means that you take your brush, with only a little paint on it, and work lightly and horizontally across the vertical line so that the painted strip blends into the unpainted strip.

E

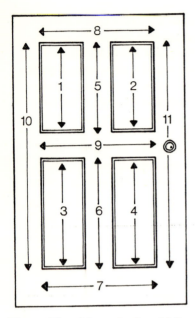

Fig 30 The right order in which to paint a panel door.

When you have finished, do clean your brushes and roller very thoroughly.
If you are stopping work for a short time for a rest and a cup of tea,
you can put the brush into a jar of turpentine, or better still, suspend it
on a string, so that it is hanging above the jar into the turpentine.

And when you have completed the job, and are putting your brushes and
roller away until next time, clean the brushes well with turpentine or
turps substitute, then wash them in a solution of detergent and dry them
thoroughly on a piece of rag. Put the brushes on one side to allow them
to dry completely before you store them away.

Wallpapering is slightly tricky, and it is useful to have a willing friend
and the right equipment.

The equipment you will need consists first of a pasting table (if there is a
hire firm in your locality, you may be able to hire a long trestle table
for a few days). Otherwise a long dining table will do, but you must cover
it thoroughly with plenty of newspaper. Then you will need a pair of
steps for use when hanging the paper, and although you could probably

hire these too, steps are a useful investment, because they are essential for all kinds of household tasks, such as hanging curtains and fixing hooks. You will also require a bucket for paste, a brush for pasting, a wallpaper brush for smoothing out the paper on the wall (available from any do-it-yourself shop); wallpaper scissors (these are extra large scissors for cutting the paper, and are a good buy if you plan to do a lot of decorating). And these complete the essentials. You will also need a ruler, which you probably have already, and a plumb line to make sure that the paper is hung straight. This you can make yourself with a length of string tied round a stone.

It is best to choose a fairly plain paper for your first attempt, because it is difficult enough to ensure that the paper hangs straight without having to fuss about matching patterns at the same time. Make up the paste as directed. There are plenty of good proprietary pastes on the market, specially made for papering, so it is false economy to try to make do with home-made flour and water paste. It is difficult to prevent home-made paste going lumpy, and you won't get such a smooth, finished result.

Cut the lengths required. It is a good idea to prepare several at a time, making sure that you allow at least 2in at the top and 2in at the bottom, which you will trim off in due course. Unroll each length on the table. Don't be afraid to use plenty of paste. A mistake that amateurs often make is not to use enough paste, and as a result the paper simply won't stick to the wall.

After you have pasted each length, you should draw the top length towards you then fold it back again on itself as if you were pleating, but letting the folds lie loosely. (See Fig 33.) If you are using a washable paper, you must put it on the wall right away, but ordinary papers can be left to soak before putting on the wall.

When you start to paper, you must make sure that you begin with a straight line, otherwise you will find the paper hangs squint as you continue round the room. This is where the plumb line comes in. Let it hang from a height and mark the line where it hangs. Even if your walls are not straight, you must follow this line.

Always paper away from the light—that is, start at a window and work round towards the door. If you are starting from the left, and for most

people this is easier, you must always work to a line on the left, so that
the edge of your paper is straight against the last edge on the
left. Use your plumb line to find the first vertical against the window edge,
and start from there.

Take the paper over your arm, and unfold the top piece leaving two
inches overlap at the top of the wall. Now hold the top of the paper with
both hands and the weight of the paper should drop straight down to
the bottom. Do not try to place the paper on the lower part of the wall
until you have made sure that it is straight and correctly placed at the
top. If the willing friend is at the foot of the steps, do not allow him or
her to grab the end of the pasted length at this stage and hold it firmly in
place. This is the surest way to tear the paper, and it is also certain to
cause friction between you.

WALLPAPERING

*Fig 31   Stages in papering a room. Begin at A, work to door, then begin
         again at C. Use plumb line at A to make sure all subsequent
         lengths hang straight.*

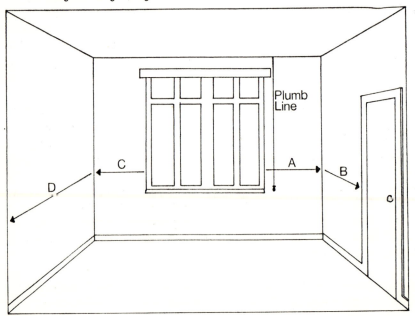

Fig 32 Paste the paper on a long trestle table.

Fig 33 Fold the pasted paper into concertina folds.

Fig 34 Make sure the first piece hangs straight. Use a plumb line.

The role of the willing friend, and roles can of course be reversed, if he or she turns out to be more skilled than you, is to watch to see that the paper is correctly placed at the top and gently guide it into place against the line on the left. When you are both certain that the paper is quite straight against the vertical line, you take the wallpaper brush and, working horizontally and vertically, smooth the paper with firm strokes so that you can, if necessary, shift it very slightly into place. Only when you are absolutely sure that the paper is correctly placed do you trim off the pieces at top and bottom, using a sharp knife.

When you reach the corners, try to avoid finishing a length right at the join. Make sure you turn the corner and press the paper firmly into the join, then start off again on the next length, once you have turned the corner.

One thing that worries amateur decorators a lot is the number of air bubbles that appear under the paper, once it is on the wall. Quite often these bubbles take a day or two to dry out, and there is nothing to get alarmed about—and absolutely no need to rip the paper off and start again!

Fig 35 Use a wallpaper brush to smooth out any bubbles.

The new pre-pasted vinyl papers are very easy to use. You simply put the cut lengths into a tray of water, soak thoroughly and then hang, and there is none of the messy business of pasting. They are ideal for amateur decorating, but these papers tend to be rather more expensive than the ordinary kind, so you will want to include this extra cost in your budget when planning the room.

If you have never papered before, it is a good idea to have a trial run in an unobtrusive spot—say inside a walk-in cupboard, using an odd length of wallpaper. Nearly everyone has lengths of paper left over from wallpapering, and friends and relatives will probably be only too willing to let you have the remains of their rolls. Once you have successfully pasted a length or two inside a cupboard, you will feel much more confident about tackling the papering of a room.

9 THE EXTRAS

When you are setting up home, there is little enough left over for extras. Even buying a lampshade or two can make a sizeable dent in your budget. But the most attractive homes I have seen were those in which the owners had used flair and imagination instead of money to add the extra touches that give a home personality.

So this chapter is about the next-to-nothing cost of adding the extras. Of course, these extras are very much a matter of personal taste, and the important thing is that it should be your taste which emerges, not that of the furnishing store.

Pictures are one of the best ways of adding personality to your home for little cost. Obviously you can't afford to go out and buy expensively framed prints, so you must make do with substitutes until you can afford to buy pictures. Anyway, your taste will probably change by then, and it is fun to switch around prints and posters to suit your mood and furnishing colours.

Here are a few cheap and easy ways to display prints and posters.

Use black or brown art paper to mount postcards which you collect from museums and art galleries. One of the most artistic displays I've seen was of postcards, which were silhouettes on a white background, themselves grouped together and pinned on to dark brown art paper. You could fix the mount to the wall with drawing pins or special picture pins which don't leave a mark.

Don't discard sheets of beautiful wrapping paper. For a small outlay you can cover a blank space on a wall or the back of a door.

Perhaps you are interested in wild flowers and have a few pressed from
a collection made on holiday. Making flower pictures is very easy. All
you need is a sheet of strong white card (art dealers sell this), and some
wallpaper paste. Lay the flowers and leaves on the paper first, working out
your grouping, and when you are satisfied with the arrangement, paint
the back of each flower or leaf with the paste and glue it down. Wallpaper
paste is good for this because it doesn't show the marks as heavy glues
do. Ferns press particularly well, and they look good in a feminine
room such as a bedroom.

You can make attractive wall pictures or panels too with dried flowers
such as everlasting flowers and honesty. If you haven't a garden, it is
possible to buy these quite cheaply. I was given one picture of everlasting
flowers and leaves in creams and browns, effectively mounted on a
piece of natural silk material. I've also seen everlasting flowers arranged
most artistically on a long strip of deep blue hessian to make a wall panel.

Don't throw out old greetings cards. I've seen these displayed very cheaply
and most attractively, glued to the rough side of a piece of hardboard.
You can often find offcuts of hardboard sold for a few pence at do-it-
yourself shops.

It is a good idea too, to look out for any posters and prints which you
can pick up cheaply. Often these may be slightly reduced in price if they
are a little marked. Instead of expensive framing, you can frame them
yourself quite easily, with glass cut to size and passepartout. It is useful
to buy a glass cutter, if you plan to do a lot of home framing. These cost
about 15–20p.

Don't discard anything that might make a picture. You can use
photographs, old sheets of music, pieces of material, embroidery, even
poems. I know of one home-owner who has added real personality to her
sitting-room with hand-lettered poems, maxims, anything that takes her
fancy. It helps if you are artistic, of course, but even typewritten poems
and quotations are better than blank walls.

What about the other extras—lampshades, cushions, etc.? The cost of
buying these ready-made can add up alarmingly, and it takes only time to
make these yourself. It isn't difficult either. Quite a lot of the work can
be done while sitting in front of the television set.

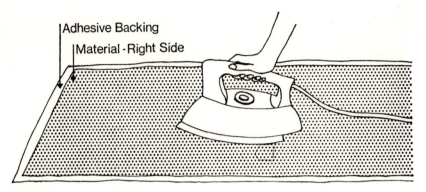

Adhesive Backing

Material - Right Side

MAKING LAMPSHADES

Fig 36   Material can be pressed on to adhesive backing.

You can make a lampshade in an evening, by using sheets of adhesive
material which are sold especially for this. All you do is iron on your
material or piece of wallpaper on to the adhesive paper. The best type of
frame to use is the drum shape. Measure the circumference of the frame,
then cut your piece of adhesive material this length and the depth of
the frame, allowing a little extra, say an inch, for the overlap. Now you
simply lay your chosen fabric or wallpaper on to the sticky side, press
heavily with a hot iron and the material sticks to the backing. Now put it
on to the frame, using a couple of clothes pegs to hold the material
firmly. Sew the shade to the frame at the top and bottom, using a thick
linen thread and a strong needle, and overlapping stitches.

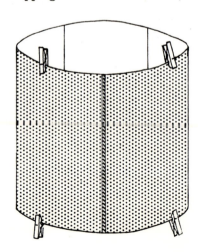

*Fig 37   Clothes pegs hold the
material to the shade.*

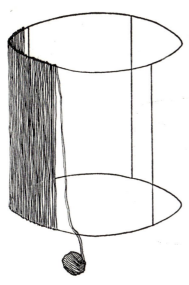

Fig 38 Dishcloth cotton can be wound vertically round the shade. Use a drum shape.

To join the ends use a little glue, and then stitch down the join. For a neat finish, use lampshade trimming, bobble fringe or piping cord around the top and bottom of the shade and down the join. When you are making a lampshade the proper way, you must cover the frame, but for the instant method it isn't necessary.

For beginners, the drum shape is best—it is easy to get into difficulties when using fluted or conical shapes. Another reasonably cheap way to make an instant lampshade is to use a drum shape and dishcloth cotton. Start at the bottom of the frame and fix the cotton firmly to the frame with a couple of knots. Then you simply keep winding over the top and down to the bottom, over and over again, keeping the cotton close to the last length until the frame is completely covered. This can look very expensive and will last for years.

Another good way to make an expensive-looking lampshade is to buy a very cheap shade, preferable slightly transparent (a thin paper shade is good for this). Then you glue flowers and leaves inside so that when the lamp is lit, you have the shape of the flowers showing through. The flowers and leaves should be pressed first, and again wallpaper paste is best for fixing because it doesn't show any marks, though any light-based glue will do. Try to choose flowers and leaves which have distinctive shapes, e.g. ivy.

Fig 39   Leaves and flowers can be used on a transparent shade.

Making cushions costs next to nothing, and once you have made your own, you will never want to pay shop prices again. It is very easy to make ordinary square cushions. It's simply a matter of stitching up three sides of a square and leaving the fourth to be finished by using press studs or Velcro, or you can stitch it if you want a permanent finish.

If you are slightly more expert, you can make fitted cushions with piping and seams. This takes a little more time, but it is well worth it and it gives your cushions a most professional look.

Felt and hessian are both useful materials for extras. For example, you can make an expensive-looking circular French cloth for a table, using brightly coloured felt. A bright orange or yellow looks good with a modern scheme. To make sure that you get the cloth exactly circular, cut out a pattern first in newspaper or a large sheet of brown paper. You can tell if the pattern is even by folding it in four and trimming the circular base until it is even, and not a lopsided arc. Then you put the pattern on to the felt and cut out the circle in felt.

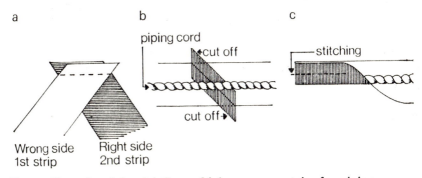

Fig 40   *To make piping (a) Cut and join crossway strips for piping. (b) Lay piping cord along the centre of strip. (c) Stitch close to the cord.*

There is no need to sew round the edges, but a white bobble fringe adds to the finish and makes the cloth look more expensive.

You can drape the cloth over any circular table—the cheaper and shabbier the table the better because it will of course be completely covered by the felt. If you are handy, you could always buy a circular top of hardboard and fix it to a base. The felt should drape to the floor, hiding the base or the legs of the table.

Don't put too many ornaments on the top. This table is simply for display, so it is best to show off a pretty ornament without cluttering the table. For example, a deep tawny orange felt could be the background for a pottery mug filled with marigolds, a shining brass lamp or an old oil lamp, polished up. On a deep pink cloth, you could put a pretty china cup filled with pink and white flowers or a white china bowl with a flowering plant such as a cyclamen. A yellow cloth could be complemented by a teak bowl, filled with oranges, lemons or nuts.

The felt will cost you about £1·25 a yard, but this is about 72in wide so it
goes quite a long way. (If you don't want to use felt, a summery printed
cotton cloth would also look effective, trimmed with matching bobble
fringe.)

If you have any scraps of felt left over, you could use these to
cover offcuts of hardboard. Cut the felt to allow for turnings of about 2in
all round. Place the felt on the hardboard and glue down on the back
of the board so that the felt neatly covers the front and the corners are
carefully mitred on the reverse. Then use a good strong glue to place a
print or postcards on the felt, so that the felt acts as a mount for the
picture.

To hang, you can use hooks with adhesive backing, which you will find
at most good stationers' and art supplies shops, and these are useful as
long as you don't attempt to hang anything too heavy.

Some effective ways of using felt are as follows : you could use black and
white theatrical prints against a deep red background, postcard
reproductions of pen and ink drawings against a coffee or deep cinnamon
background, flower pictures or prints of birds against deep sage green.
Of course, it is wise to choose only cheap prints for this scheme, because
they are difficult to remove from the felt once you have glued it down, so
can be used in one colour scheme only.

And what adds the final extra touch to your home is the miscellaneous
collection on the shelves, which shows that you, that is, a person of your
particular tastes, have set your personality on the room. Books, china,
souvenirs, anything can be displayed on a couple of shelves, and no
matter how small your home, do try to leave space for display. Otherwise
your home becomes just a show room, lacking in any personality. The
Victorians went too far—often their rooms were just a claustrophobic
clutter. Today we have gone too far in the other direction. Anything that
could be remotely called 'junk' is swept out to the dustbin. It seems
very unfortunate that today, when faceless conformity is all too common,
you can often go into a home, and find not a single clue to the
owner's character.

So don't throw out all the clutter. Train your eye to search for things
that you will enjoy looking at and handling. It doesn't matter what they

are. The criterion should be that they give you pleasure. One of the most attractive displays I've seen was set out on a natural wood shelf. It was a collection of acorns and autumn leaves, with a grouping of stones of unusual shapes, most of which had holes through the centre. They looked like a Henry Moore family of stones, but were in fact picked up on Beachy Head. Rock bottom cost, in fact.

10 THE FRONT DOOR

Bringing personality to your home begins at the front door. There is no use in working out a considered scheme indoors if the entrance is bleak and uninviting.

If you are lucky, you may have a small front garden and porch. This gives you a great deal of scope. But perhaps yours is an upstairs flat with an entrance which is just one of several doors in a passage. Here you are certainly more limited, but there is still a lot you can do to make your entrance different from all the others.

I'm assuming that the reader's first home is a flat or a modest maisonette, or perhaps a newly converted basement, rather than the semi-detached or detached house. So let's begin at the basement and work upwards.

There are a great many basement first homes, especially in London and large cities where space is at a premium and land is valuable.

The outlook from a basement is often sunless, and if this is your problem, the answer is white and lots of it. Suppose you look on to a north-facing yard, then you could paint the whole yard in white, using whitewash or distemper on the walls. You could fix white-painted wooden trellis to the wall that gets most sun, that is the one facing south. You could then use this trellis to take climbing plants which are not choosy about being in full sun for the whole day, because even if you put your trellis on a south-facing wall, you won't get a great deal of sun in a basement yard. Suitable climbers would be a passion-flower (I once saw a splendid one climbing rampantly in a sunless patio just behind Oxford Street in London) or a Russian vine, or ivy. If your back yard is entirely paved, you will have to take up paving stones to plant the climbers, and make sure that their roots are about 10in away from the wall, or no moisture will reach the roots and they will become too dry. You could

Fig 41 Tubs and hanging baskets can make a basement look attractive.

also plant your climbers in tubs, but it is important to make sure that they have enough moisture, and plants in tubs need feeding continuously.

If your back yard is entirely without sun, then you could probably grow successful ferns, but you would have to be choosy about the type of plants you put in tubs or boxes. Catmint, primulas, pansies and nasturtiums do quite well without being too fussy.

F

Fig 42 Flowers in tubs and boxes add character at ground level.

If your front door leads on to the typical basement exit of stone staircase with iron railings, then you could make use of the area by painting it white and hanging baskets of flowers, say two or three along the area. Petunias, geraniums and tradescantia are good choices for town baskets. So are fuchsias and trailing lobelia. Stocks and pansies are less happy. Make sure that baskets get plenty of moisture and take them down for watering at least once a week, when they should be given a good soak.

You could put a tub at the foot of the steps and train a vine or other rampant climber up the railings (and you can buy at most gardening shops a harmless dog and cat repellent which will keep animals away).

It is a good idea to match the front door to the colour scheme—or to choose a neutral colour which will not quarrel with vivid plants.

Fig 43 Trellis and climbers give interest to an ordinary front garden.

Even if you decide not to have plants, you can still use colour imaginatively to give an impression of light and space. The colours you select depend on whether your tastes are modern or traditional, but don't let 'traditional' mean safe and dull. Aim for subtle greys and blues, or a warm brick red against black and white paintwork would be another effective scheme. If you want something more modern, you could have an acid yellow front door against black and white paintwork, or a door painted in bright tangerine or deep plum.

Coming up a flight, you may have a small modern home with a tiny front garden. If your house is part of a planned development, then it is

*Fig 44   Any front door can be improved with colour and use of
          plants and flowers.*

probable that your front door will look exactly like all the others, and you
will be forbidden by the terms of your lease to do anything too drastic
to it. Your problem is how to make your front door look quite different
from all the others without radically altering the structure.

You can do this by adding trellis to plain brick walls and growing
climbing roses, or winter jasmine, or clematis, or something similarly eye-
catching. You could add a bracket and a hanging basket to one side of
the front door under a porch. You could place a green painted tub to one
side of the front door, and fill it in spring with bulbs, and with petunias
and geraniums in summer. Even a tiny patch of garden no more than 3ft
square can give scope for carrying out imaginative colour schemes. An
all-yellow scheme for spring could have yellow crocuses, followed by
daffodils, yellow auriculas, primroses, and in summer interesting bedding
plants such as a mixture of yellow petunias and yellow pansies. These
summer bedding plants are very easy to grow and can be raised from
seed, sown in trays indoors and put out in a sunny window until they are
large enough to plant out.

It is surprising how grouping and colour planning can make even a small
border look unusual and attractive. Recently I saw a minature front
garden with groups of daffodils and a few clumps of early yellow
polyanthus with—an unusual touch—plants of silver striped foliage in
between.

And I remember another house, much grander, with a hyacinth blue front
door, where they had a wonderful spring bedding scheme of blue and
white hyacinths, white narcissi, and later deep purple tulips and clumps
of forget-me-not. (It was rather a grand house, for the colour scheme was
completed by a Silver Shadow Rolls Royce standing at the front gate!)

But back to budget colour schemes. If your front door has glass panels,
it adds warmth to have door curtains in the hall, and you can use these to
bridge indoor and outdoor colour schemes. We have already mentioned
some ideas in the chapter on furnishing the hall. It certainly helps to
carry the harmony theme right through from the front door. For
example, you could have a coffee-coloured front door, white paintwork
outside, door curtains in a pink and brown mosaic print, one wall in
the hall papered in the same pattern (use a matching fabric and wallpaper),
and three remaining walls of the hall painted in a soft pink, with white
woodwork.

Going further up, we come to the first floor and beyond. Your front door
may open on to a fire-escape type staircase, or it may be on to a landing
and yours is one of several doors, all identical. But it is still the entrance
to your home, and should speak your personality, just as much as the
more obviously individual front door at ground level. Unless your lease
stipulates that all the doors must be painted exactly the same (and
how unimaginative can landlords get—they might as well decree that we
should all dress the same!) then there is nothing to stop you painting
the front door any colour you like.

If the door is panelled, then why not try painting it in two colours, or one
vivid colour and white. You could use sage green on the top, middle,
side and centre panels, then fill in the inset panels with white. Or you
could contrast a soft pink and magnolia, grey and white, or deep coffee
and white. Or you could use a thin border of black with yellow or black
and orange or brown and orange. For a front door on its own, simply set in
a corridor of emulsion-painted walls with no surround such as brick or
stone to take the harshness from a vivid colour, it is probably best to
stick to a fairly quiet colour; otherwise the bright door may jar in time.

A quiet colour needn't be insipid, though, as the subtle greens and blues
show. Try to get your effect by using very simple accessories— say a
pale yellow door with a brass knocker well polished, or a china name plate

(there are many which are well designed) against a blue door, or an expensive-looking door handle. You can do a lot with gold spray paint —I know of one young householder who went wild with gold spray and covered everything, including some family heirloom china figures. The first visitor who arrived looked like Midas because the householder had sprayed the door knob and forgotten to put up a 'wet paint' sign.

A front door upstairs with a borrowed light may have a recessed window panel of frosted glass and this gives you a chance to display hanging plants.

It is worth while spending a little time over the design of your entrance; after all, it is the first clue that your new neighbours and friends will have to the kind of person who is living next door to them. And there is nothing like imitation! There is a remarkable little street in Hampstead in north London, which must have been a real neighbourly effort, for each door is painted in an individual shade—soft violet, sage green, pearly grey, all blending and toning so perfectly that the scheme must have been carefully planned.

Perhaps your scheme can't be so perfectly conceived, but one well-designed front entrance can stand out in a row of conformist doors. Your ideas may even spread until everyone in the row is thinking in terms of new colours and you may have started a modest revolution.

11 VALUE FOR MONEY

Buying and furnishing a house is an expensive business, and your troubles aren't over when you have paid the final removal bills.

There are lots of traps for the inexperienced home-owner, and when money is scarce, it can be heart-breaking to make a mistake in a purchase, to find that you have wasted precious savings on something that didn't wear well, or turned out to be an item of furniture that you didn't really want.

It is tempting, when you move into a new home, and need carpets, furniture, curtains and all sorts of things, to think that easy-payment hire purchase is the answer to all your furnishing problems. But before you decide to buy on hire purchase, it is important to sit down and work out just how much it will cost you. The total payments on an item of furniture will be more than the cash price; on a large item the total can be quite a bit more than the cash-down cost. In other words, you are paying for the privilege of borrowing and having the goods to use now.

You have to be very sure, before you buy on hire purchase, that you aren't going to regret the buy, and that you really want the goods sufficiently to pay more than the cash price. You must be sure too, that you can afford the repayments. Two or three pounds a month may not seem a great deal now, but if you also have to pay mortgage repayments, electricity and gas bills, ground rent, rates, water rate, and perhaps a telephone bill as well, then the two or three extra pounds a month can be the last straw.

I'd advocate H.P. only when you are absolutely certain that you are going to save money this way. For example, if you are working all day, and can shop only at lunch time and at weekends, a small refrigerator bought on hire purchase could mean a considerable saving on food bills. If

you own a refrigerator, it means you can shop wisely and cheaply once
a week and prepare soups, casseroles, pudding toppings and flan cases,
put them in the refrigerator and save pounds on tins and instant meals
bought in the delicatessen on the way home.

Or, if you want to save money by making curtains, sheets, cushions and
other things for your home, a sewing machine bought on H.P. would
be a money-wise investment.

Perhaps you have a job that involves constant washing of overalls, or
maybe you have a young family. Then it might be worth while working
out if you would save by buying a washing machine or a small spin
drier, on hire purchase. How much do you spend at the launderette? Do
you wash once a week, and do you use the ordinary machine or the family
wash machine? How much do you spend on driers? Would it be more
economical to buy a washing machine or a spin drier on hire purchase?
These are the sort of facts and questions you want to think about before
you consider whether to buy on H.P. or not. Work out a few sums too
—and don't forget to allow for depreciation and possible repairs to
the machine after the guarantee period has ended.

If you do decide to buy a cooker, refrigerator or washing machine or
anything of the sort on hire purchase, it is advisable to go to a reputable
store, to your local dealer, or to a gas or electricity board showroom.
Remember to read the agreement carefully, and be sure that you ask any
questions before you sign.

You may, from time to time, be offered something such as a refrigerator
cheap by someone who 'knows the trade'. However tempted you may be,
remember that such offers don't carry any guarantee, and if the
refrigerator breaks down during the first week, there is nothing you can
do about it. In any case, it is foolish to buy goods if you don't know
exactly where they come from, or why they are being sold cheaply. The
sale may be genuine sale of old stock or the goods may have,
as they say, 'fallen off the back of a lorry', in other words, be stolen.

How, in the bewildering maze of consumer goods on sale in the shops, can
you be sure that you are spending your hard-earned cash on something
that will stand up to wear? Every new home-owner can tell tales of
disappointing purchases, but fortunately the law and the consumer
protection groups can help you considerably.

You can help yourself too, by being bright and wide-awake when you are shopping. For example, if you are buying fabrics, make sure that the store supplies adequate instructions on washing or dry cleaning the fabric. If in doubt, ask. The assistant should know, and in large stores usually does, but if you have any difficulty, ask to see the buyer, and don't be satisfied with a hesitant 'it ought to wash all right'.

It is the same with equipment. Make sure that any piece of equipment carries adequate instructions, ask for a demonstration, and if you don't understand the leaflet you are given, go back to the shop and ask the assistant or the manager to explain. Many manufacturers still couch their instructions in terms that only a computer expert could understand. If the information still seems mystifying, write to the manufacturers and tell them so. And if you think a piece of equipment is badly designed, or unsafe, or just plain inefficient, it is also worth getting in touch with the manufacturer, or with your local consumer group. Many areas have these excellent groups and the public library will be able to give you the address of your local branch.

Of course, it takes time to complain and follow up a complaint about an unsatisfactory buy, but it is important. No one will think you are being over-fussy and pernickety if you expect good value from a buy, and when you are furnishing a first home, you cannot afford to waste hard-earned money.

There are, however, ways and ways of complaining. It is no use stamping into the shop and browbeating the poor assistant who, after all, didn't make the saucepan whose handle fell off. It's better to ask to see the manager or his assistant and explain the situation to him. A more-in-sorrow-than-in-anger, 'I'm sure you want to help' attitude will get you much further. It's wise to keep it cool and civilised, and remember that the store manager does want to help you because a dissatisfied customer is a poor advertisment.

Sometimes, however, you may not be able to get satisfaction from the store, and then it is certainly worth while writing to the manufacturer direct with a copy of your letter to the store.

The law protects you too, by the Trade Descriptions Act. The Act is specially designed for the benefit of the consumer. If a trader makes untrue statements about the goods or services he is offering he is liable to be fined or imprisoned.

For example, if a trader displays goods as 'all wool' and they are a blend of wool and cotton and only 10 per cent wool, then he can be fined. The same applies to prices. A shopkeeper who marks goods 'reduced from £x. . . .' must have charged the old price for at least 28 days in the last six months, unless he makes it very clear to the contrary.

There are other ways in which traders can infringe this Act. A trader who 'knowingly and recklessly' makes false statements or claims about accommodation or services he is offering is liable to prosecution.

If you think that a shop or trader is infringing the Trade Descriptions Act, then you can inform the local weights and measures inspector whose address you can find out from the Town Hall or from your local library. The weights and measures authority will look into the question of infringement. You may not get your money back, but your action will help other people.

Having furnished your home, how can you make sure that your house is fully protected against fire or damage by flood or any other disaster? It is very important that your home should be fully insured.

If you are buying your home through a building society or insurance company loan, then you will already have an insurance policy to cover the building against fire and perhaps some other risks. This is one of the conditions that societies make before they lend money.

Perhaps you are a tenant, and your landlord is responsible for insuring the building against fire, flood and similar disasters.

Whether you buy or rent, you ought to make sure that the contents of your home are adequately insured.

As a house-owner, you can have a buildings and contents policy in one.

This covers fire, lightning, explosion and certain other kinds of damage to the structure of the building *and* your possessions inside. It includes losses through theft or attempted theft from the premises.

Or you can have a separate contents policy for your personal possessions. The contents policy covers the same risks, but applies to your household goods and personal effects only, such items as books, clothes, furniture and radios.

Some companies offer a special 'flatlet' policy to tenants. If you live in a flat where the landlord is responsible for the insurance of the building, then the 'flatlet' policy may suit you, but it is worth checking to see if a normal 'contents' policy would be more suitable. The landlord's policy does not cover loss or damage to your own possessions, so you must make sure that they are adequately covered.

How do you know that you are insuring the contents of your home for the right sum? The best way is to make a list of everything you own. Estimate how much the main items cost when new, and then deduct something for wear and tear. On the other hand, remember to make allowances for any particular items—maybe a piece of jewellery or a small antique you have been given—which may have increased in value.

You cannot insure for normal wear and tear or depreciation, and if you buy a piece of furniture, say a chair, for £20 today, and its value in ten years' time is about half, then £10 is all you could expect to recover if the chair were destroyed in a fire.

Normally your insurance company will send you a reminder each year when the premium is due, but it is under no obligation to do this, and you ought to check for yourself each year to see that the premium is paid and your possessions are insured for the right amount. You may have bought quite a few new items since the previous year, and perhaps you have made one very large purchase, such as a piece of electrical equipment. Don't forget to include it in your new total and to increase the premium if necessary.

How much will it cost? The average premium per £100 of contents is about 25p, but this varies from one company to another. Some companies offer a no-claim bonus too. If the sum insured is very low, you may be charged a set premium, as small insurances are not really economic to the insurer.

It's worthwhile reading a very useful booklet called *Everyday insurance* which was prepared by the British Insurance Association for the National Citizens' Advice Bureaux Council. The booklet includes many helpful answers to the kind of questions people ask about household insurance. Details about how to obtain the booklet are in 'Where to find out about. . . ', p. 99.

12 TAKING MEASUREMENTS

It isn't difficult to calculate how much wallpaper you will need, how much emulsion and gloss will cover your walls and paintwork, or how much material will be required for curtains. It it worth while taking time to measure properly. Once you know exactly the quantities you need, you can shop with more confidence. You won't have the disappointment of finding that you can't, after all, afford the attractive material that you liked in the sample or the deflating experience of discovering that the curtains you have made won't fit your window.

It is always better to err on the generous side when measuring and buying. Rather have a little wallpaper left over, which you can use to cover a wastepaper basket or lampshade, than be half a yard short of paper; and better to use up extra material for matching cushions than have to skimp on curtain fabric. It is usually very difficult to get an exact match of wallpaper, paint or fabric. This is not the stockist's fault; it just happens that in manufacture one bolt of material may differ in weave ever so slightly from another. The shade of paint from one consignment may also be very slightly lighter or darker. You cannot guarantee that you will get exactly the same batch of paper or bolt of material on your second visit to the shop, so it is important to buy the proper quantity to begin with. Before you begin papering or painting, you must measure the room.

First, you measure the height in feet from the skirting board, then you measure right round the room horizontally, taking in the doors and windows. Don't measure the ceiling. It is difficult to measure a ceiling anyway, and the quick calculating table will give you a pretty good idea of the amount of paint required for the ceiling, based on the other measurements. Most wallpaper stockists will help you calculate, but here for reference is the way to estimate how much paper and paint you will need.

WALLPAPER

Height in feet from skirting	Distance in feet round walls													
	30	34	38	42	46	50	54	58	62	66	70	74	78	82
7–7½	4	5	5	6	6	7	7	8	8	9	9	10	10	11
7½–8	5	5	6	6	7	7	8	8	9	9	10	10	11	11
8–8½	5	5	6	7	7	8	9	9	10	10	11	12	12	13
8½–9	5	5	6	7	7	8	9	9	10	10	11	12	12	13
9–9½	6	6	7	7	8	9	9	10	10	11	12	12	13	14
9½–10	6	6	7	8	8	9	10	10	11	12	12	13	14	14
10–10½	6	7	8	8	9	10	10	11	12	13	13	14	15	16

Number of rolls required

EMULSION

Height in feet from skirting	Measurement in feet round walls												
	28	34	40	46	52	58	64	70	76	82	88	94	100
7	3	4	4	5	6	7	7	8	9	9	10	11	11
8	4	4	5	6	7	8	8	9	10	11	11	12	13
9	4	5	6	7	8	8	9	10	11	12	13	14	16
10	5	5	6	7	8	9	10	11	12	13	14	15	16
11	5	6	7	8	9	10	11	12	14	15	16	17	18
Ceiling	1	1	2	2	3	3	4	5	6	6	7	9	10

Amount in pints—two coats

GLOSS

Measurement in feet round walls, including
doors and windows

	28	34	40	46	52	58	64	70	76	82	88	94	100
Amount in pints—one coat	1½	1½	1½	1½	2	2	2	2	2	2	2½	2½	3

Most paint is now sold in litres. Your dealer could help with conversion or you could work it out for yourself (1 pint = 568 ml; 1 litre = 1·76 pints).

Although the paint quantities are quoted in pints, remember that it is more economical to buy in bulk, and a gallon will cost you less per pint than the small pint can. If you know that eventually you want to paint all the paintwork in your flat white, it would be economical (if you can afford it, and have the storage space) to measure all the paintwork now, reckon how much you will need and buy in bulk. You needn't worry about the keeping qualities of paint. As long as you replace the lid firmly on an open tin after use, and make sure that no dust or dirt gets into the tin, then the paint will remain in good condition for a very long time.

If your neighbour or a relative happens to be painting at the same time, then it might be worth while working out just how much you both need and placing a bulk order with a local firm. The firm might not offer you discount at the beginning of the spring painting season, but if you are painting out of the season and give the firm a large enough order, they might well agree to allowing you discount—especially if they are clearing stock ready for next year's supplies.

CURTAINS

Measuring for curtains is not difficult.

First you measure the length of the curtain track. If your curtain track is already in place, you will probably find that it extends about 9in on either side of the window to allow you to pull the curtains back. So you measure the width of the window, plus nine inches on either side, that is 18in extra in all. Allow 2in for each side seam, and 1in for each middle seam required.

Fig 45 Measurements you will need for curtains.

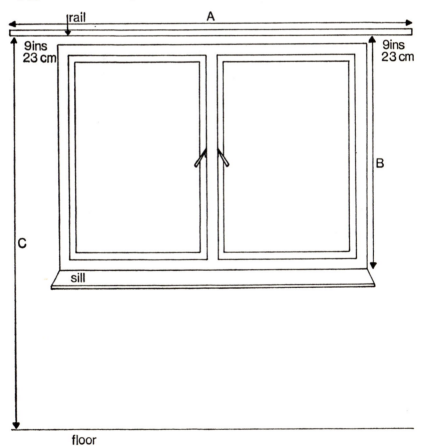

Now decide on the length of the curtains. If your window sill is less than
2ft from the floor, it is a good idea to choose floor-length curtains.
Consider the proportion of your windows, too. If you have modern picture
windows, then short curtains, finishing just below the sill, would look
best. If you have a French window with small windows on either side,
you might choose long curtains, so that you can draw them right across
door and windows and make a wall of curtaining (not expensive if
you choose an economical fabric, such as repp).

Long curtains should clear the floor by about 1in and you should allow
3in for the bottom hem and 4in for the heading.

Short curtains should finish about 3–4in below the sill. Again you allow
3in for the hem and 4in for the heading.

How do you decide how many yards of material you need? Curtain
materials are usually made in 48in widths. You will have to allow enough
material for fullness in the curtain, and obviously light fabrics, such as
nets, will have to be fuller than heavier materials.

If the length of your curtain track (measurement A on the plan) measures
up to 5ft, then 1 width will be enough for each curtain. If A measures
from 5–7ft you will need 1½ widths for each curtain. If A measures
over 7ft you will need 2 widths for each curtain.

For very light fabrics, such as nets, you will need 2 widths in any case,
and for medium-weight fabrics, it is wise to choose 1½ widths, even if
your length of curtain rail is less than 5ft.

You have already measured the length from rail to sill or floor. Now you
multiply the length by the number of widths, divide by three to get the
number of yards, and that is the quantity of 48in wide material you will
need.

Width = A (window width + 18in + 6in for hems)
   If A =
   up to 5ft you will need   1 width of 48 in wide material
   5ft to 7ft   1½ widths of 48 in wide material
   over 7ft   2 widths of 48 in material
Length = B (length to sill + 3in hem + 4in heading)
     or C (length to floor + 3in hem + 4in heading)

Material required $\dfrac{\text{Widths} \times \text{length}}{3}$ for each curtain

Multiply by 2 to get total required for pair of curtains.

If you are making curtains for a main room, such as a sitting-room or bedroom, it is better to line them if at all possible. Lining helps to keep the heat in, and it also means the curtains will hang better.

It is best to buy your lining material when you buy the curtain fabric. You will require the same amount of lining material so remember to allow for this when estimating the cost. There are many different materials suitable for lining, and it is a good idea to ask the advice of the assistant in the store. It is very important that the lining should be washable.

CARPETS

LENGTH	6'0"	6'6"	7'0"	7'6"	8'0"	8'6"	9'0"	9'6"	10'0"	10'6"	11'0"	11'6"	12'0"
Width **7'6"**	5	5½	6	6¼	6⅔	7¼	7½	8	8⅓	8¾	9¼	9⅔	10
9'0"	6	6½	7	7½	8	8½	9	9½	10	10½	11	11½	12
10'6"	7	7⅔	8¼	8¾	9⅓	10	10½	11¼	11⅔	12¼	13	13½	14
12'0"	8	8⅔	9⅓	10	10⅔	11⅓	12	12⅔	13⅓	14	14⅔	15⅓	16

LENGTH	12'6"	13'0"	13'6"	14'0"	14'6"	15'0"	15'6"	16'0"	16'6"	17'0"	17'6"	18'0"
Width **7'6"**	**10½**	11	**11¼**	**11⅔**	**12¼**	**12½**	**13**	**13⅓**	**13¾**	**14¼**	**14⅔**	**15**
9'0"	**12½**	**13**	**13½**	**14**	**14½**	**15**	**15½**	**16**	**16½**	**17**	**17½**	**18**
12'0"	**14⅔**	**15¼**	**15¾**	**16⅓**	**17**	**17½**	**18¼**	**18⅔**	**19¼**	**19**	**20½**	**21**
10'6"	**16⅔**	**17⅓**	**18**	**18⅔**	**19⅓**	**20**	**20⅔**	**21⅓**	**22**	**22⅔**	**23⅓**	**24**

The above table is by courtesy of The British Carpet Centre.

If you are buying a carpet, you ought to get a proper estimate from the store, and the store will also arrange the measuring and fitting of your carpet. But it does help when you go shopping to have a rough idea of how many square yards you will need, and the table on the previous page is an approximate guide. The widths are the standard broadloom widths, but you can also have a carpet made up from body widths, which are woven in 27in and 36in widths.

13 TOOLS

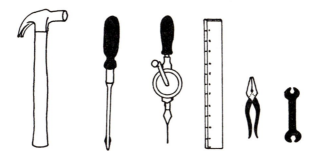

Fig 46 A selection of tools: claw hammer, screwdriver, drill, ruler,
pliers and spanner.

Any do-it-yourself job is made ten times easier if you have the right tools,
and it is poor economy to make do with such substitutes as a blunt
knife and a pair of scissors. You can buy quite good quality tools from
any chain store, and it is certainly an investment to build up a small
collection of the basic tools so that you are equipped to tackle any do-it-
yourself job.

Here is a list of the basic tools I suggest the new home-owner might buy.

SCREWDRIVERS
One large and one small (although you can never have enough screwdrivers
and it is a good idea to collect several of different sizes).

DRILL
This needn't be a power tool. A small hand drill, available for little cost
from any chain store, will be enough for first do-it-yourself jobs.

SPANNER
Essential for any amateur plumbing jobs, such as undoing the nut on a waste pipe when the sink is stopped up.

PLIERS
CLAW HAMMER
NAILS AND SCREWS OF ALL SIZES

GOOD-SIZED RULER OR FOOT RULE
You will need this for measuring—an inch tape is not the same for it will stretch in time.

GLASSPAPER
Buy several different grades. This is very useful when you are preparing old furniture for repainting or smoothing down Polyfilla after filling in cracks.

Also worth collecting are:
SCREW TOP JAM JARS
Useful for storing nails and screws. If you are short of space, the lids could be glued to the roof of a cupboard or fixed to clips, and the glass jars screwed on.

CONTAINERS FOR MIXING
Yoghurt and cream cartons are handy for mixing Polyfilla.

OLD BRUSHES
Any old toothbrush can be saved. Such brushes are very useful when you are stripping furniture, as they help you to reach out-of-the-way corners.

14 BOOK LIST

This is a short list of some books I have found useful. Of course there are many more excellent books on furnishing and decorating which will help you. You will discover a good selection at your public library. Books on home-making are usually classified at 644–5, books on gardening under 635. A look round the library shelves will give you an idea which books you want to buy and keep for your own reference.
There are plenty of weekly and monthly magazines too, all of which have helpful home features, and the staff are always willing to advise readers.

And don't forget that a number of firms will let you have, for the price of a stamped, addressed envelope, some of their informative literature which makes excellent reading.

Finally, it's a good idea to start a home notebook of your own and paste in any cuttings about new furnishing fabrics and wallpapers, and note sources of information, ideas that you have copied from friends' homes, anything that will come in handy. You may not be furnishing yet, but, when you do plan your own home, or even re-furnish one room, the ideas you have collected will make planning very much easier.

GENERAL
Good Housekeeping's *Running a home is fun*, Margery Edwards and Gillian Smedley, Ebury Press. Written especially for domestic science classes, but bright and interesting and full of ideas for all age groups.

Enjoy Face-Lifting your Home, Gladys Williams, Gollancz.
A lively, informative guide to replanning a home, but just as valuable for new home-owners.

House into Home, Elizabeth Kendall, Aldine paperback.
Not written specially for budget home-makers, but full of good ideas that can be copied inexpensively.

Better Home Management, Aileen King, Mills & Boon.
Specially useful for advice on fabrics, their choice and care.

CURTAINS, COVERS, UPHOLSTERY
Curtains to Covers, Margaret Marchant, Evans.
Soft Furnishings Made Easy, Anne Blythe Munro, Methuen.
Soft Furnishing, Joanne Prior, Bell.
Modern Upholstery, Dorothy Cox, Bell.
All these books are helpful guides to the technicalities of furnishing.

DECORATING
Home Decorating, Harry Ratcliffe, Mills & Boon.
Written by an expert, but simple enough for beginners in decorating.

GARDENING
The Small Garden, C. E. Lucas Phillips, Pan.
Window Box Gardening, Xenia Field, Pan.
Enjoy Making a Garden out of Nothing, C. A. Lejeune, Gollancz.

All full of good ideas on plants, shrubs, bulbs and ways to brighten the
outlook at your front door.

MONEY
Money Wise, Gilda Lund, Mills & Boon.
Low Cost Homes to Rent or Buy, J. E. M'Kenzie-Hall, Robert Hale.
The legal side of buying a house (England and Wales), Consumers'
Association.
The law for consumers, Consumers' Association

For more advanced home-owners
House conversion for Everyone, Gladys Williams, Robert Hale.

15 WHERE TO FIND OUT ABOUT...

DESIGN
The Design Centre, 28 Haymarket, London SW1Y 4SU. A permanent
display of well-designed goods, and a useful reference section. In other
parts of the country there are Design Centres in:

Glasgow: 72 St Vincent Street, Glasgow C2
Liverpool: Liverpool Building and Design Centre, Hope Street, Liverpool.
L1 9BR.
Manchester: 115 Portland Street, Manchester. M1 6FB.
Southampton: The Southern Counties Building and Design Centre,
Grosvenor House, 18–20 Cumberland Place, Southampton, SO1 3BD.
Bristol: Stonebridge House, Colston Avenue, The Centre, Bristol, 1.
Nottingham: The Midland Building and Design Centre, Mansfield Street,
Nottingham, N91 3FE.

Sanderson's, Berners Street, London W1, have beautifully designed room
sets, displaying their papers, paints and fabrics, and showing many ideas
which are worth copying.

If you live in or near London, don't miss the Furniture Show which
is usually held in February at Earls Court. The room sets in the
model houses are well worth seeing. The Ideal Home Exhibition, held in
March, is good for do-it-yourself ideas.

BUILDING MATERIALS
The Building Centre, Store Street, London WC1 has a permanent
exhibition of building materials, flooring etc., and a helpful information
desk where you can obtain leaflets and addresses of firms.

There are Building Centres in other parts of the country which can
provide similar help and information.

Coventry: The Coventry Building Information Centre, Council House, Earl Street, Coventry CV1 5SE.
Dublin: The Building Centre of Ireland, 17 Lower Baggot Street, Dublin 2.
Liverpool, Manchester, Nottingham, Southampton: See under Design Centres above.
Glasgow: 6 Newton Terrace, Glasgow G3 7PF.
Stoke-on-Trent: The Building Information Centre, College of Building and Commerce, Stoke Road, Shelton, Stoke-on-Trent, ST4 2DG.

CARPETS
The British Carpet Centre, Dorland House, 14–16 Lower Regent Street, London SW1.
A showroom full of carpet samples, and an advisory service. Readers outside London can receive literature and advice by post or telephone.

BEDDING
The National Bedding Federation, 251 Brompton Road, London SW3 issues seven very helpful consumer leaflets, which are available free of charge (for a stamped, addressed envelope). The Federation will also give advice on bedding.

DYEING
Dylon International Ltd., 139–51 Sydenham Road, London SE26 have a very good consumer advice bureau and supply on request a number of excellent leaflets. They advise on dyeing, will test fabrics and advise on colour matching.
Drummer Dyes, manufactured by Roberts' Croupline Ltd., Croft Lane, Bolton, Lancs. offer a helpful leaflet on the use of their product, free on request.

FABRICS
Dralon: The Dralon Information Bureau, 100 Wigmore Street, London W1, has a number of useful leaflets on the care and washing of Dralon fabrics.
The British Man-Made Fibres Federation, Bridgewater House, 58 Whitworth Street, Manchester M1 6LS, issues a booklet *Facts about man-made fibres.*
Linens, cotton, towelling, candlewick, etc., by the yard: Limericks, Hamlet Court Road, Westcliff-on-Sea, Essex. Catalogue on request. Cotton sheeting in plain colours and candy stripes, candlewick, towelling etc., by the yard. Postage 12p on a complete order (U.K. and Ireland rate).

Hessian: Russell and Chapple Ltd., 23 Monmouth Street, Shaftesbury
Avenue, London WC2. Leaflet and samples on request. Mail order service.

GLASS AND MIRRORS
The Glass Advisory Council, 6 Mount Row, London W1Y 6DY produces a
number of leaflets, available to the public on request, including a very
attractive booklet, *The Verity Book of Decor and Design*. These leaflets
give a great deal of help on the choice of mirrors and their use in the
home.
The Glass Manufacturers' Federation, 19 Portland Place, London
W1N 4BH, will also advise on glass in the home.

HEATING
The National Heating Centre, 34 Mortimer Street, London W1N 8AR.
The Centre does not sell fuel or equipment, so can give impartial advice
about heating. Literature by post costs 10p minimum, and for written
inquiries there is a fee of £1.

HIRE PURCHASE
A useful leaflet on hire purchase, *Hire-purchase: What you need to
know* . . . is published by HMSO and available from Citizens' Advice
Bureaux.

HOME DECORATING
Polycell, Broadwater Road, Welwyn Garden City, Herts. offer a lot of
excellent advice on home decorating problems and are always glad to help
customers. They produce some attractive laminated cards on Stripping
Paint and Polish, the Polycell Handyman Range, and other informative
topics.

Formica Ltd., Dept PR, P.O. Box 2, De la Rue House, 84–86 Regent Street,
London W1R 6AB, or local branches of Formica, will advise on using
Formica products.

HOUSECRAFT
The Electrical Association for Women, 25 Foubert's Place, London W1,
runs simple courses in electrical housecraft for the public each spring and
autumn in London. In three one-hour lessons you can learn to wire a
plug, read a meter and replace fuses. The Association has branches

throughout the country and will arrange courses where there is a special demand. The Association also has a Home Electricity Certificate, which can be taken in schools.

HOUSEHOLD PESTS
Rentokil Advice Centre, 16 Dover Street, London W1. Free advice and a useful information sheet.

LAUNDERING
The Home Laundering Consultative Council, 41–2 Dover Street, London W1X 4DS, issues a leaflet about home laundering, but cannot advise on washing problems.

INSURANCE
Everyday insurance, a booklet produced by the British Insurance Association, is available from Citizens' Advice Bureaux.

WISE BUYING
The Consumers' Association, 14 Buckingham Street, London WC2. Publishers of the invaluable consumers' magazine, *Which?*, Motoring *Which?*, Money *Which?* and Handyman *Which?*
A subscription to *Which?* for 12 monthly issues costs £2·50 (and of course you can see back numbers at your local library).

The Consumers' Association also publishes a number of excellent booklets (see book list), and these are available to anyone, whether subscriber or not. Available by post from Consumers' Association Subscription Department, Caxton Hill, Hertford, or if you live in London, you can call at the Association's main offices at 14 Buckingham Street, London WC2.

INDEX

Acrylic emulsions 59
Auctions 28–9

Basement yard, decorating 76–8
Bathroom 55–7
Bedding 39–42, 100
Bedroom, furnishing 34–43; plan for 13
Beds, choosing 34–35
Bedspreads, making 41–2
Blinds, roller and Venetian 54
Blue, colour schemes using 14
British Carpet Centre 32, 100
Brushes, care of 62; choosing 59
Building Centres 99
Buying Secondhand 21

Cabinet, medicine 56; orange-box 56; whitewood 37–8, 53
Candlewick 40, 100
Carpenters 52–3
Carpeting 32, 34, 44, 100; measuring 93–4
Chairs, basket 42; bentwood 22, 42; dining 22; re-upholstering 27–8; stripping and painting 22–8
Chest of drawers 39
Colour schemes, planning 10–17, 44
Consumer protection 84–5
Consumers' Association 102
Cookers 53, 84
Cracks, filling 58–9

Cupboards, built-in 35, 36; home-made 51–2, 53; whitewood 36
Curtains 19–20, 48, 54, 55, 81; lining 93; measuring for 91–3
Cushions 28, 72

Design Centres 99
Dining alcove, plan for 12
Doors, painting 61–2, 76, 78, 80, 81–2
Dyeing 20, 100

Electrical Association for Women 9, 101
Electricians 53
Emulsions 58, 60; amount needed 89
Everyday insurance 87

Fabrics 18, 19, 21, 100
Feathering 61
Felt 72–3, 74
Flooring 29, 32–3, 44, 53
Floors, sanding 29–31
Furniture, buying secondhand 21–2, 28–9; stripping and painting 22–8; whitewood 35–8

Gardens 79–81
Gloss 58–9, 60, 61; amount needed 90
Green, colour schemes using 15–16

Haircord 32–3, 34, 44
Hall 44–5

Hardboard 53, 69, 74
Heating 101
Hessian 20, 28, 72, 101
Hire purchase 83-4, 101
Home-made units 51-2
Housecraft, electrical 101-2

Insurance 86-7, 102

Kitchens 49-54

Lampshades, making 70-2
Laundering 102
Living-room, plan for 11;
    furnishing 18-33
Locks 48

Mattress ticking 42
Mirrors 39, 101

Orange boxes 18, 45, 56

Paint, amount needed 89-90;
    choosing 58-9; how to 60-1;
    mixing 16-17; preparing walls
    for 58, 59; rollers 59, 60
Paste, wallpaper 63
Pegboard 53
Pests, household 102
Pictures, displaying 11; flower 69;
    framing 69; mounting 68, 74;
    substitutes for 48, 68, 69, 74
Piping 73
Plants, indoor 57; outdoor 76-8,
    80
Plastic foam 28, 56
Plumb line 63, 64
Polyurethane gloss 24, 36, 59
Pre-pasted vinyl wallpaper 67

Quilts, continental 42

Rawlplugging 45-8
Ready-made units 50-1

Red, colour schemes using 15
Refrigerators 53, 84
Repp 19, 20, 28
Re-upholstering 27-8
Rollers, paint 59-60
Rugs 32, 44
Rush matting 32

Safety 54
Sales 21
Secondhand buying 21-2
Sheets, making 40
Shelving 39, 45
Sofas 28
Sponges, making 56
Staining wood 25
Storage space 35, 56

Table, dining 22, 73; dressing 34,
    39; bedside 34, 39
Tablecloths 73
Tools 95-6
Towelling 55-6, 101
Trade Descriptions Act 85-6

Umbrella stand 45
Underlay, carpet 32

Varnishing 25
Velvet 20
Vinyl flooring 53

Wallpaper, hanging 63-7; pasting
    63-65; pre-pasted vinyl 67;
    rolls needed 88-9; washable 55,
    63
Weights and Measures Inspector
    86
Wet edge 61
Whitewood furniture 35-8
Woodworm 22-3

Yellow, colour schemes using 16